THE SMART STUDENT'S GUIDE

TO SMART MANUFACTURING AND INDUSTRY 4.0

OR FOR OTHERS SEEKING AN UNDERSTANDING OF THE NEW MANUFACTURING PARADIGM

2021 EDITION

TEXT AND ILLUSTRATIONS BY MIKE NAGER

Published by Industrial Insights LLC
New Jersey
www.industrialinsightsLLC.com

INDUSTRIAL INSIGHTS
LLC
PUBLISHING AND CONSULTING PARTNERS

ISBN-13: 978-1-7363625-0-1 E-Book
ISBN-13: 978-1-7363625-1-8 Paperback

Library of Congress Cataloging-in-Publication Data
Library of Congress Control Number: 2021930111
Our publications are available at special quantity discounts for use in sales promotions or in educational training programs.

To join our mailing list and become eligible to receive a free chapter of a future publication, register at
www.industrialinsightsLLC.com

To shoot us a message or interesting story related to manufacturing, send it to
SmartStudents@industrialinsightsLLC.com

Twitter: @Ind_Insights

LinkedIn: https://www.linkedin.com/company/industrial-insights-llc/

TABLE OF CONTENTS

Preface: A Fresh Look at Manufacturing 7

Acknowledgments 12

Disclaimers 13

SECTION I:
CURRENT STATE OF MANUFACTURING IN USA **15**

Chapter 1: The Elephant in the Room – Manufacturing
          Job Losses 16
    Effect of Automation 18
    Discussion Topics 20

Chapter 2: Manufacturing Today. 22
    Automation is Not the Enemy 23
    Discussion Topics 24

SECTION II:
TWO REASONS MANUFACTURING IS IMPORTANT **25**

Chapter 3: Manufacturing and National Defense 26
    Vulnerabilities in the Supply Chain 29
    USA Manufacturing Institutes 29
    Discussion Topics 31

Chapter 4: Manufacturing for Wealth Creation
          and Distribution 32
    The Manufacturing Multiplier Effect. 33
    Discussion Topics 34

SECTION III:
ABOUT MANUFACTURING AND BUSINESS **35**

Chapter 5: Manufacturing Industries and Processes 36
    Discussion Topics 39

Chapter 6: Internet of Things, Industrial Internet of Things,
Industry 4.0 – I'm So Confused 40
How IoT, IIoT, and Industry 4.0 are Related 41
The Four Industrial Revolutions. 42
Discussion Topics 46

Chapter 7: What Xactly is XaaS? 47
Everything as a Service?. 49
Discussion Topics 51

SECTION IV:
ENABLING TECHNOLOGIES: THE HARDWARE GADGETS
AND GIZMOS 53

Chapter 8: Industrial Networks and Cybersecurity 54
Networks 54
Cybersecurity in the Industrial Plant. 57
Movies that Feature Cybersecurity 59
Examples of Careers in Industrial Control Systems and Cybersecurity . . 60
Discussion Topics 61

Chapter 9: The Rise of the Robots. 62
Industrial Arms 63
Mobile Robots. 64
Collaborative Robots (or Cobots) 64
Movies that Feature Robotics. 65
Careers in Robotics. 66
Discussion Topics 67

Chapter 10: A Little Bit Here, A Little Bit There: Additive
Manufacturing Matures 68
Subtractive vs. Formative vs. Additive Manufacturing 69
Movies that Feature Additive Manufacturing 72
Careers in Additive Manufacturing 73
Discussion Topics 73

Chapter 11: Sensor Prices Are Falling Down, Falling Down,
Falling Down. 74
Wireless Communication Ability 76
Energy Efficient 76
Networkable. 77

Smart 77
Monitoring 78
Alarm, Control, and Prediction 78
Movies that Feature Smart Sensors 79
Careers in Sensors 79
Discussion Topics 80

SECTION V:
ENABLING TECHNOLOGIES: STODGY SOFTWARE
AND COOL APPS **81**

Chapter 12: Big Data and Visualization of Information 82
The Five "V"s of Big Data 82
Movies that Feature Data and Big Data 84
Careers in Big Data 84
Discussion Topics 85

Chapter 13: Skip the Drugs, Alternative Realities
    Are Already Here 86
Augmented Reality 86
Virtual Reality 88
Movies that Feature Augmented and Virtual Reality 89
Careers in Augmented and Virtual Reality 89
Discussion Topics 90

Chapter 14: Artificial Intelligences Begin Their Ascent 91
Other Names for Artificial Intelligence 92
Movies that Feature Artificial Intelligence 96
Careers in Software and Artificial Intelligence 96
Discussion Topics 97

Chapter 15: Digital Twins Mirror Reality 98
Types of Digital Twins 99
Movies that Feature Digital Twins 101
Careers in Digital Twins 101
Discussion Topics 101

Chapter 16: Blockchain:
    Applied Mathematics to Keep Us Honest 102
Blockchain to Fight Counterfeiting 103
Movies that Feature Blockchain 104

Careers in Blockchain. 105
Discussion Topics 105

Chapter 17: Software Rules 106
Computer-Aided Design (CAD) 107
Computer-Aided Manufacturing (CAM) 107
Enterprise Resource Systems (ERP) 108
Manufacturing Execution System (MES). 108
Product Lifecycle Management (PLM) Software. 109
Process Control and Automation Software 110
Customer Relationships Manager (CRM). 110
Careers in Software. 111
Discussion Topics 112

SECTION VI:
FINAL THOUGHTS ON THE HUMAN ELEMENT 113

Chapter 18: Soft Skills Never Go out of Fashion,
        But You Have to Keep Up 114
Critical Thinking Skills 115
Movies that Feature Soft Skills 116
Careers in Soft Skills 117
Discussion Topics 117

Chapter 19: Getting into Manufacturing 119
The Four-Year University Degree 120
The Two-Year College Degree 121
Plant Floor Approach: Right Into the Workplace 122
Networking 123
Discussion Topics 124

Conclusion 125

Further reading recommendations 128

About the author 130

Endnotes 132

PREFACE:
A Fresh Look at Manufacturing

If you are a student in the United States, there is a good chance that you are not considering a manufacturing career in your future. You probably don't have close friends or family working in the industry and few popular shows feature it. My advice is, do not overlook it!

This book will introduce you to exciting career opportunities that smart manufacturing provides today. It's why I capitalize it in this book: Smart Manufacturing.

Manufacturing suffers an image problem due to decades of failed national policies that allowed U.S. manufacturers to move to other parts of the world. With the ensuing closures of many factories, local and state communities experienced much hardship. This history of the manufacturing industry has created a deeply negative impression. What parents would encourage their children to work at the company that laid off Grandpa after thirty-seven years of service and avoided paying his pension?

Adding to this common wisdom among most Americans, a few facts further depress the image of manufacturing.

First, the overall number of people working in U.S. manufacturing has been declining. The reason is that around the year 2000, national policies adopted a global supply chain philosophy that manufacturing didn't have to exist within U.S. shores.

Second, the number of people working in manufacturing as a percentage of overall jobs is currently the lowest in U.S. history.

Third, manufacturing output as a percentage of gross national product is also at its lowest point in history.

But are those negative headlines and perceptions the whole story? Consider another fact. Manufacturing output, which is essentially the amount of goods made in America, rises every year. The U.S. now produces more products than at any other time in history.

Smart Manufacturing, also referred to as Industry 4.0, is starting to shake up the previous worldwide business model of off-shoring manufacturing operations to areas with low labor rates *by making labor rates less relevant*. Smart Manufacturing is growing. You have an opportunity to join the industry as it reinvents itself.

In the past, the picture that manufacturing conjured was a large number of people lined up to perform manual and often repetitive tasks all day long. The operations could be simple, such as inserting one material into another, or complex, such using a lathe to shape a spinning metal piece. If you search for pictures of manufacturing online, you are likely to find black and white photos of huge plants with hundreds of workers shoulder-to-shoulder at work. Unlike these depictions, manufacturing today evokes very different images.

Smart Manufacturing refers to the most modern way of making entities involving automated and high-tech devices developed with advanced technology. Do you like to play video games? The software engines that display game graphics are also utilized in manufacturing. Do you text on a smartphone? That technology is used for machines to communicate with other machines. These are just two examples. Industry 4.0 is the term that the world uses to describe the revolution of manufacturing created by technology.

The COVID-19 pandemic provided a wake-up call for the world as supply chains proved to be shockingly fragile during this worldwide crisis. The result has been an acceleration of reshoring efforts in the U.S. Factories that were taken offshore decades ago are being brought back given the benefit of manufacturing and supply chain management being in close proximity. It is expected that two million or more jobs could be created within the next seven years.

This book will provide you with a unique viewpoint to identify manufacturing opportunities you may not have considered. I will lead you through an exploration of how Smart Manufacturing works and the specific technologies that *you* could focus upon for a career. The following is a snapshot of each section in the book.

Section I: Current State of Manufacturing in the USA

In this section, I describe the widespread misconceptions about manufacturing that negatively influence decisions to pursue a career in the field. Government policies, especially at the federal level, exacerbate the perception that manufacturing is a dying occupation, causing many people to avoid recommending or pursuing careers in the industry. In contrast to the prevailing beliefs, I then describe how modern manufacturing incorporates cutting-edge technologies in clean, safe, and sophisticated facilities.

Section II: Two Reasons Manufacturing is Important.

In this section, I explore the national interest issues regarding domestic manufacturing, specifically its importance for wealth creation and national defense. These concerns are beyond that of just simple commerce and profit considerations of the private sector. It is my belief that these issues will accelerate manufacturing investments and will drive a new wave of employment and business opportunities.

Section III: About Manufacturing and Business

In this section, I list the main types of manufacturing industries according to the government classification system. There is a wide variety of products described that require varying production methods depending upon what is being made. Smart Manufacturing is a new term that communicates the modern approach to all production methods. I organize what can be confusing terminology in a way that you will find clear and concise. Smart Manufacturing means producing things in a smart manner but also creating smart devices. These smart devices are blurring the lines between what is a product and what is a service. In doing so, new business opportunities are being created for those who understand what customers truly want when buying a product or service.

Section IV: Enabling Technologies: The Hardware Gadgets and Gizmos

In this section, I introduce the physical devices that provide the automation capability of a modern manufacturing plant to run efficiently. The topics I discuss are all key parts of the modern factory. Industrial Networking and Cybersecurity involve securing data transfers within the enterprise and to customers and suppliers. Robotics involve automated "muscle-power" that reduce the need for human workers to perform highly repetitive physical tasks. Additive Manufacturing, sometime referred to as 3D printing, is advancing so rapidly that changes will occur before you even finish reading this book. The technology that enables the designer to create a part with only a computer file and some raw material is revolutionizing entire manufacturing and service industries.

Section V: Enabling Technologies: Stodgy Software and Cool Apps

In this section, I explore the advances in software that are just as important as the hardware in powering Smart Manufacturing operations. Big Data drive important decisions on the plant floor on a real-time basis and at the "Top Floor" where business and investment decisions are made at the executive level. I discuss Augmented and Virtual Reality as they are incorporated into both smart products and Smart Manufacturing factories. Artificial

Intelligence provides automated "Brain Power" to reduce the need for human workers to perform highly repetitive mental tasks and, instead, to concentrate on more creative aspects. Digital Twins, the capture of a physical item or process into a computer simulation, is an important emerging technology. So is Blockchain, the ability to provide traceability and ensure authenticity of manufactured items. I finish out this section with Software Rules by listing many types of software platforms that rule the manufacturing facility.

Section VI: Final Thoughts on the Human Element

In this concluding section, I discuss the people part of Smart Manufacturing. While the technologies are impressive and "sci-fi-like" in their sophistication, people play the most important role in manufacturing. The chapter on Soft Skills highlights the importance of human creativity and the ability to form and function in highly effective teams. The final chapter provides tips on how to get started in a Smart Manufacturing career.

With the ubiquity of search engines, information is never far from reach so I have kept easily found information out of the book. I have identified a few book references that stand out and so I offer them to you for further reading. Shoot me an email at SmartStudents@industrialinsightsLLC.com if you find one that didn't make the list.

ACKNOWLEDGMENTS

A big thank you goes out to the following:

To all those guiding others to be their better selves, no matter their age or path in life.

To all those spending their own time writing books, articles, blogs, and LinkedIn posts to educate others, often for no compensation except the satisfaction of helping others.

To my employers, customers, clients, and colleagues who allowed me to experience the marvels of manufacturing firsthand.

To my parents, Regina and Bruce, who encouraged me and my sisters, Kathy and Jennifer, to follow our own paths and provided support all along the way.

To my daughters, Julia and Kelsey, who were my real-life student avatars so I could visualize my target audience while I was writing.

And to my wife, Laura, who patiently listened to me during this longer-than-expected book writing experiment and provided encouragement all along the way.

DISCLAIMERS

FROM THE AUTHOR

The following disclaimer applies to any content in this book:

This book is commentary intended for general information use only and is not investment advice. Mike Nager does not make recommendations on any specific or general investments, investment types, asset classes, non-regulated markets, specific equities, bonds, or other investment vehicles. Mike Nager does not guarantee the completeness or accuracy of analyses and statements in this book, nor does Mike Nager assume any liability for any losses that may result from the reliance by any person or entity on this information. Opinions, forecasts, and information are subject to change without notice. This book does not represent a solicitation or offer of financial or advisory services or products. This book is only market commentary intended and written for general information use only. This book does not constitute investment advice. All links were correct and active at the time this book was published. All content is the personal opinion of Mike Nager and does not necessarily represent any view or position held by any past or current client or employer.

FROM THE PUBLISHER

The following disclaimer applies to any content in this book:

SECTION I:
CURRENT STATE OF MANUFACTURING IN USA

Chapter 1:
THE ELEPHANT IN THE ROOM – MANUFACTURING JOB LOSSES

"The rumors of the demise of the U.S. manufacturing industry are greatly exaggerated."

— Elon Musk, Founder of Tesla

Nothing discourages someone from considering or recommending manufacturing as a career more than the relentless job losses the U.S. manufacturing sector has faced for thirty years. I attribute this to the passage of the North American Free Trade Agreement (NAFTA) in the 1990s.

NAFTA accelerated the manufacturing offshoring movement and the creation of a global supply chain accelerated America's job losses. U.S. corporations were allowed, perhaps even encouraged, by federal government policies to relocate manufacturing to areas of the world with low labor costs. Industries and companies that relied extensively on labor had an incredible incentive to move their operations without penalty. Public policymakers were unwilling to stem the exodus of manufacturing and didn't seem to think it was important. Consider the following quote from an official at that time:

"America's role is to feed a global economy that's increasingly based on knowledge and services rather than on making stuff."[1]

— *Lawrence Summers, senior U.S. Treasury Department official during the Clinton administration*

Many people warned what would happen as a result of these policies. Consider Ross Perot, the billionaire founder of Electronic Data Systems, who ran as an independent candidate in the 1992 presidential election. During his three-way debate with George H. W. Bush and Bill Clinton, Perot famously turned on a vacuum cleaner on stage and stated that the "giant sucking sound" would be the sound of jobs leaving the U.S. if the North American Free Trade Agreement (NAFTA) was approved by Congress.

"We have got to stop sending jobs overseas. It's pretty simple: If you're paying $12, $13, $14 an hour for factory workers and you can move your factory South of the border, pay a dollar an hour for labor,...have no health care — that's the most expensive single element in making a car — have no environmental controls, no pollution controls and no retirement, and you don't care about anything but making money, there will be a giant sucking sound going south... when [Mexico's] jobs [will] come up from a dollar an hour to six dollars an hour, and ours go down to six dollars an hour, and then it's leveled again. But in the meantime, you've wrecked the country with these kinds of deals."[2]

— *Ross Perot. Third Party Candidate in 1992 U.S. Presidential Election*

Proponents of NAFTA pointed to East Asia's rising economic competition and the powerful European Union coming into existence as economic threats. Having access to low-cost labor in the western hemisphere could counter these new competitors.

Manufacturing left the United States in droves, just as Perot had predicted. And although wages didn't go down, they didn't go up either, resulting in more than twenty years of salary stagnation for the middle class. And the jobs didn't go to just Mexico, where Perot had noted a 6:1 labor rate advantage over the U.S. Some went to China, whose labor rate advantage was more than 26:1, which defeated NAFTA's purpose in the end because manufacturing didn't have to be in the region, it could be anywhere in the world.

There is a ripple effect when manufacturing leaves an area. Drive through the Rust Belt of the Midwest and a few surrounding states and you will see that when manufacturing departs, so do the suppliers and service providers. Real estate prices depreciate as workers and their families seek employment elsewhere. With a declining population, retail shops and restaurants close.

Consider this quote from a life-long Ohioan:

> "We're losing all kinds of white-collar jobs, all kinds of jobs in addition to manufacturing jobs, which we're losing by the droves in my state."
>
> — *Sherrod Brown, U.S. Senator from Ohio and former U.S. Representative and Ohio Secretary of State*

Effect of Automation

Automation has a major impact on manufacturing jobs. With automation, some jobs become obsolete and disappear forever whereas others are created. For example, you may never have seen someone hand-washing clothes in bulk, but you may know individuals involved in washing machine repair. A skilled repair person has a considerably higher value job than any human clothes washer did in the past.

In the 1800s, America's top industry was agriculture, employing nearly 70% of all workers. As mechanization increased farming productivity, fewer workers were needed to grow food. Today, less than 2% of the U.S. population is involved in agriculture. Surnames like Farmer and Smith originated in workers' professions. Hardly anyone today can trace their surname to their family's original profession.

My family tree undoubtedly had many tailors when they selected the surname of Nager and though there continue to be many tailors in the world, my family is not among them. These historical work connections to our heritages have always changed as new technologies emerged.

The figure below shows job titles that have been eliminated or created by technology. As a student, I urge you to focus on the ones in the circle on the right. It is the responsibility of the individual, education system, and society in general to move people's skills to where the jobs are.

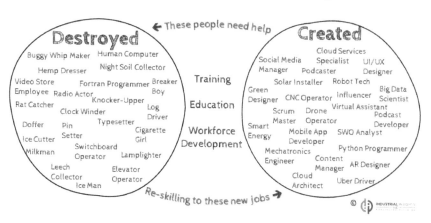

An industrial revolution changed agricultural society forever, the knowledge revolution of the later 20th century changed the industrial society, and another is happening today in Smart Manufacturing, sometimes called Industry 4.0. Positions that require little knowledge and skill have diminished in number and pay much less than positions requiring substantial knowledge and skill.

According to the Organization for Economic Cooperation and Development, up to 14% of what are referred to as repetitive jobs may disappear within the next decade and another 32% will include greater automation.[3] Job titles like social media manager did not exist in 1990, let alone a century earlier.

The bottom line is that automation may have taken away job titles while creating others, but it was inadequate and non-existent federal policies that are responsible for factories and entire industries relocating outside the U.S.

Those policies made it nearly impossible for any individual state to defend their manufacturing bases against the power of foreign governments that targeted them and an American government that seemed resigned to seeing them go.

Mechanization dramatically reduced the labor needed to produce sustenance levels of foods and automation is doing the same for manufacturing. In this book, I will show that automation creates far better jobs and opportunities and manufacturing is worth considering when deciding upon your career path.

Discussion Topics

Find statements from local, state, and federal politicians and characterize their manufacturing industry views.

1. Describe how the tone is different depending on the level of the officeholder's position.

2. Which political party seems to support manufacturing more than the other, and what makes you think so?

3. Which political party seems to support specific manufacturing industries more than others, and what makes you think so?

4. What types of automation do you witness in everyday life that may have been done manually in the past?

Chapter 2:
MANUFACTURING TODAY

"The right focus for the U.S. is on advanced manufacturing —
something that requires innovation."

— *Tim Cook, CEO of Apple*

It's common in the U.S. for manufacturing operations to be defined
by a series of adjectives starting with the letter "d" such as dirty,
dangerous, dumb, dull, and deafening. These certainly describe
what some manufacturing was like many years ago. It wasn't until
the Occupational Safety and Health Administration (OSHA) was
established in 1970 that workplace conditions changed for the better.
Before that, it was estimated that 14,000 workers were killed and
over two million were injured every year. OSHA and other changes
made the workplace much safer.

These laws work. I was involved in a project with a USPS distribution
center that was unable to open because the noise from its miles of
conveyors was too high to be safe. We identified a much quieter
technology that required more automation. When we finished, we
had a much safer facility that also saved a considerable amount
of electrical energy. This is one of the seldom discussed aspects
of Industry 4.0. Highly flexible and modern manufacturing plants
create benefits in many other areas, including energy savings, safety,
and environmental gains.

Automation is Not the Enemy

Automation continues to evolve in making manufacturing more efficient. Parts that were previously hand-made are now machine-made. Machines that relied on humans loading and unloading parts now have robots doing that work. If you visit a modern manufacturing facility, you will find operations that are sleek, clean, and full of cutting-edge machinery, equipment, and systems. There are automated gantry systems, mobile robots, and collaborative robots communicating with a software manufacturing execution system in real-time.

In the previous chapter, I discussed policy decisions that caused the total number of manufacturing jobs to drop in America. Highly manual, labor-intensive positions moved overseas to take advantage of cheap labor. But what if manufacturing doesn't need cheap labor to produce a product? If not, where would manufacturing be located? Close to inexpensive energy sources? Close to transportation hubs? Close to skilled workers? Close to customers?[4]

American Giant, a sweatshirt manufacturer, decided that ensuring tight quality control and rigorous inventory management was the key to success. That's why they opened up operations in North Carolina and later won Fast Company's #38 Most Innovative Company in 2015. They created an Internet shop where customers expected fast delivery, a new business model at the time, and increased their presence in the U.S. by also purchasing American cotton.[5]

We are going to see more of these decisions as Smart Manufacturing takes hold. The problem with changing perceptions about the industry is that only a small portion of the U.S. population has direct experience with a modern manufacturing facility. They have never seen a medical implant manufacturer using industrial robots that feed a tool to create a customized artificial knee out of machined titanium. Or a semiconductor plant where the cleanroom requirements are so stringent that only super-conducting, non-contact conveyors are used to gently float the product to work cells without any friction to create dust.

The Smart Manufacturing workplace often looks like a set from a science fiction film or from a NASA control center. In later chapters, I will explore how the modern manufacturing plant utilizes innovations in hardware and software platforms to create highly sophisticated and "cool" workplaces as well as great career opportunities for those with the right skills, abilities, and mindset.

Discussion Topics

The topic of manufacturing is in the news as shortages of products from N95 masks to cleaning wipes continues into 2021, several months after the COVID pandemic started.

1. Find three current articles in newspapers, magazines, or online about manufacturing and discuss similarities and differences in what you learned in this chapter. Describe the tone as negative, positive, or neutral.
2. Explain why "d"-word adjectives about manufacturing are no longer valid.

SECTION II:
TWO REASONS MANUFACTURING IS IMPORTANT

Chapter 3:
MANUFACTURING AND NATIONAL DEFENSE

"The Pentagon now manufactures in secure facilities run by American companies only about 2 percent of the more than $3.5 billion of integrated circuits bought annually for use in military gear."

— John Markoff, Journalist

In recent years, there has been an increasing realization that a strong national defense requires a strong domestic manufacturing base that can quickly build and reliably supply American forces. Serious shortcomings in current manufacturing capacity have been identified and there are now government policies underway to increase domestic manufacturing. These changes will lead to an increased number of companies, plants, and manufacturing career possibilities within the U.S.

Imagine if the country's defense capability — the ability to create, distribute, and deploy forces anywhere globally — was dependent upon materials and components supplied by foreign companies located in countries near or where the conflict was occurring. Imagine that those foreign governments might even own those companies and could control the logistical centers, airports, and ports used to transport materials and components to other parts of the world, including the U.S.

Well, you don't have to imagine this scenario. It has been the current state of national defense in the U.S.

Influential and powerful politicians of all party affiliations have shown that they don't understand the connection between a strong manufacturing base and a strong national defense. They have caused tremendous damage to defense capability due to their myopic view of manufacturing as a solely economic enterprise or mere private industry concern. The following quotes are a common refrain:

> "As long as China is selling us the products we need, the location of manufacturing isn't that critical for the economy."[6]
>
> — *Kenneth Green, American Enterprise Institute*

> "Potato chips, computer chips, what's the difference? $100 of one or $100 of the other is still $100."[7]
>
> — *Michael Boskin, Chair of the Council of Economic Advisors during the George H. W. Bush administration, current Professor of Economics and Senior Fellow at Stanford University's Hoover Institution.*

Even brilliant people outside the industry don't seem to understand the importance of manufacturing, specifically in the high-tech sector.

In order for manufacturing to support national defense, leaders of these companies must have manufacturing expertise. The following quote shows how much Edward Deming, the father of modern quality control methodologies, understood about the importance of leadership:

"The prevailing — and foolish — attitude is that a good manager can be a good manager anywhere, with no special knowledge of the production process he's managing. A man with a financial background may know nothing about manufacturing shoes or cars, but he's put in charge anyway."

— *Edward Deming, the Father of Modern Quality Control*

How do you think practical manufacturing knowledge advances? It's by doing manufacturing!

The difference between a potato and a computer chip goes beyond the unit price. The computer chips are required to make Patriot surface-to-air missiles, F15 integrated fighter jets, and Abrams M1 tanks work. I am not minimizing the complexity of making mass-produced potato chips. The technology and controls related to the mass production of a perishable product that requires end-to-end traceability are hardly trivial. I have many friends who work for household name food manufacturers, and they have rewarding and challenging careers.

But the manufacturing of an integrated computer chip is a whole new level of complexity, beyond the steps needed from refining the raw materials to manufacturing wafers in highly secure clean rooms. The computer chip powers the world's electronics in commercial and defense applications. The knowledge needed to make computer chips comes from working day by day in these environments, learning what works and doesn't work. It comes from realizing that your success is tightly coupled with that of your suppliers and requires intense, constant communication on a nearly daily basis. It comes from subtle process improvements that only become evident from actual measurements and experiments.

In the September 28, 2020 episode of the podcast *Sway*, Elon Musk argued that creating a product's prototype is trivial compared to scaling it to production, which is 10 to 100 times harder than building the prototype. U.S. research institutions and labs lead the world in developing concepts and even prototypes, but the real commercial value comes from making a sellable product that requires incremental modifications during which effectiveness is measured step by step.

Vulnerabilities in the Supply Chain

The outsourcing of manufacturing discussed previously has damaged the production of vital components, materials, and equipment, and eroded what we planned to excel at — the knowledge economy. The following is just a partial list of vulnerabilities in the defense supply chain that demonstrates how widespread the problem is:

▶ One supplier provides all solid-fuel rocket motors used in missiles.
▶ One supplier controls 80% of the thermal battery market used in missiles.
▶ One supplier in Belgium provides all Dechlorane Plus 25 used in weapon insulation and this supplier relies on one supplier in China for all of the chemical precursor needed.
▶ Only one rare earth mine exists in the U.S.
▶ China provides 100% of the world market share for rare earth processors.
▶ China produces 10 times more lithium than the U.S.
▶ China has 30 times more lithium reserves than the U.S.

USA Manufacturing Institutes

As half the battle in solving any problem is recognizing that there is a problem, a promising development is the recent movement toward acknowledging the situation. U.S. federal dollars have funded fourteen research centers known as the Manufacturing USA®

Institutes. They focus on advanced electronics and optics, advanced materials, advanced energetics manufacturing, and manufacturing process advancements. Eight were established by the Department of Defense (DoD), five by the Department of Energy, and one by the Department of Commerce.

The following are the eight DoD-funded institutes:

▶ **America Makes** (The National Additive Manufacturing Innovation Institute) in Youngstown, Ohio
▶ **MxD** (Manufacturing x Digital Institute) in Chicago, Illinois
▶ **LIFT** (Lightweight Innovations for Tomorrow) in Detroit, Michigan
▶ **AIM Photonics** (American Institute for Manufacturing Integrated Photonic) in Albany and Rochester, New York
▶ **NextFlex** (America's Flexible Hybrid Electronics Institute) in San Jose, California
▶ Advanced Functional Fabrics of America in Cambridge, Massachusetts
▶ **BioFabUSA** (Advanced Tissue Biofabrication Institute) in Manchester, New Hampshire
▶ Advanced Robotics Manufacturing Institute in Pittsburgh, Pennsylvania

The mission of all the institutes is to close the gap between a proven lab result or prototype and the next cutting-edge technologies to drive manufacturing dominance in the U.S. It takes a lot of time, money, and faith that any new technology will become a successful product for commercial or defense applications.

The institutes provide guidance and investors from basic research through the creation of viable products. Their initiatives may focus on funding research and development (R&D) of a new technology or helping solve the production "scaling up" problem identified by

Elon Musk earlier in the chapter. Or they may fund basic education, workforce development, or training outreach programs to increase the numbers of under-represented employee populations within the manufacturing industry.

Discussion Topics

Research and development in manufacturing is being encouraged at the federal level by the formation of manufacturing institutes.

1. Research your two closest Manufacturing USA® Institutes and discuss their recent initiatives to encourage the development of new technology.

2. Contrast and compare the focus areas for research and development, production techniques, and education initiatives funded by the two institutes.

Chapter 4:
MANUFACTURING FOR WEALTH CREATION AND DISTRIBUTION

"Not only the wealth; but the independence and security of a Country, appear to be materially connected with the prosperity of manufactures."

— *Alexander Hamilton, first U.S. Secretary of the Treasury*

Alexander Hamilton realized in 1791 that both the security of the country (discussed in the last chapter) and wealth of the country are both dependent upon a strong manufacturing base. His message was lost during the last few decades but, recently, it has re-emerged as a key issue. Discovering anew the reality that manufacturing creates widespread wealth will result in policies that support, promote, and grow opportunities in the industry within U.S. borders.

Manufacturing is one of the best forms of wealth creation as it adds value to raw materials. Moreover, manufacturing creates demand for the work of other professions, as the following quote illustrates.

"Every manufacturing job supports 3.6 additional jobs."

— *Harry Moser, Founder of the Reshoring Initiative*

The Manufacturing Multiplier Effect

The National Association of Manufacturers estimates the multiplier effect is $3.60 for every $1 of manufacturing output. The manufacturing plant needs to hire many workers and buy machinery and raw materials from suppliers. Departments of human resources, finance, operations, sales, marketing, facilities management, and product management must be created, and engineering teams need to be formed. Consulting firms, restaurants, office supply stores, and other businesses grow to support the manufacturer. Realtors, cleaners, and restaurants serve the manufacturing workforce, not the other way around.

"In every society, manufacturing builds the lower middle class. If you give up manufacturing, you end up with haves and have-nots, and you get social polarization. The whole lower middle-class sinks."

— *Vaclav Smil, Professor at the University of Manitoba*

The housing bubble illustrates this idea as during a bubble, home prices rise dramatically based on great demand, speculation, and spending. During such times, attorneys, accountants, and financial types create wealth without underlying sustainable changes in real estate values.

Because manufacturing generates wealth, it is no accident for the standard of living to rise the fastest in developing countries that concentrate on building a manufacturing base. For example, wages in China during the 2010 decade increased by 20% each year as manufacturing expanded. The declining cost advantage in China is one reason why the American Giant sweatshirt company (discussed in Chapter 2) located its manufacturing in the U.S. Though China held a cost advantage of about $7 for manufacturing, this amount was shrinking due to higher wages, higher transportation costs, and problems associated with shipping mass quantities of merchandise on slow ships.[8]

Discussion Topics

Manufacturing creates wealth not only by converting materials into higher value products, but by requiring an ecosystem of suppliers and service companies to support its operations.

1. What role should the federal government have in supporting manufacturing and why do you think so?
2. Identify a large, local manufacturer and map out a possible supply chain of raw materials into the company. Then map the output of the company to another manufacturer, sellers, or consumers.
3. Which services do you think this large, local manufacturer requires from other companies?

SECTION III:
ABOUT MANUFACTURING AND BUSINESS

Chapter 5:
MANUFACTURING INDUSTRIES AND PROCESSES

"By his very success in inventing labor-saving devices, modern man has manufactured an abyss of boredom that only the privileged classes in earlier civilizations have ever fathomed."

— *Lewis Mumford, American Historian*

Many people today would argue that they aren't bored at all and life is busier than ever. But Mr. Mumford was correct in noting that as a society, we are spending less time on jobs requiring manual labor primarily due to the various manufacturing industries.

Up until now, I have been discussing manufacturing in general. At this point, I will focus on the specific manufacturing industries and how they are classified in the U.S. The North American Industry Classification System (pronounced NAKES) used to classify the 1,000 different industries and subgroups with a long string of numbers as the identifiers.

As you see below, the first numbers define the broad category, while the subsequent numbers provide more granularity. I have detailed machinery manufacturing to six digits as an example of the greater granularity

31 Manufacturing
311   Food Manufacturing
312   Beverage and Tobacco Product Manufacturing
313   Textile Mills
314   Apparel Manufacturing
315   Leather and Allied Product Manufacturing
321   Wood Product Manufacturing
322   Paper Manufacturing
323   Printing and Related Activities
324   Petroleum and Coal Products Manufacturing
325   Chemical Manufacturing
326   Plastics and Rubber
327   Nonmetallic Mineral Products
331   Primary Metal
332   Fabricated Metal
333   **Machinery Manufacturing**
       3331   Agriculture, Construction, and Mining
       3332   Industrial Machinery Manufacturing
              333242 Semiconductor Machinery
              333243 Sawmill, Woodworking and Paper Manufacturing
              333244 Printing Machinery
              333249 Other Industrial Machines
       3333   Commercial and Services Industry
       3334   Ventilation, Heating, Are-Conditioning, and Commercial Refrigeration
       3335   Metalworking Machinery
       3336   Engine, Turbine, and Power Transmission
       3339   Other General-Purpose Machinery Manufacturing
334   Computer and Electronic Product
335   Electrical Equipment, Appliance, and Component Manufacturing
336   Transportation Equipment
337   Furniture and Related Product
338   Miscellaneous Manufacturing

What actual processes go on in these industries? They can be broadly characterized as the following:

Discrete Manufacturing produces individual items where the output is in units, pieces, or items, like one toaster oven or twelve lightbulbs. It can vary from a highly repetitive line where identical products are made with no variation in the production line at one end of the spectrum to a job shop model that just does single piece one-off type of work at the other end.

Process Manufacturing produces a liquid, powder, or gas with the amounts measured in volumes or weights, like ten pounds of sand or a barrel of oil.

Batch Production occurs when well-defined quantities of product are made at once, like a small baker making 144 cookies at once after mixing up a large batch of dough.

Continuous Production produces products without stopping and is very common in petroleum, chemical, and paper production. These processes frequently run 27/7/365 — the very definition of nonstop.

Often a combination of processes are employed in a single manufacturing facility. For example, a large commercial baker might bake its cookies in batches of 1,000, continuously mix up the dough, and have a packaging line that creates discrete boxes of cookies for sale.

Products made of metal have their own set of specific manufacturing processes.

1. **Machining** — Material is removed from larger raw stock to create a finished product by milling, grinding, turning, drilling, or polishing a larger piece. In the past, this process was done manually but today, it is completed almost entirely by computer numeric control or CNC machines. CNC machines were some of the first smart manufacturing processes that combined the functions of a machine and computer for automation in the 1970s.

2. **Joining** — Parts are attached via welding, gluing, fastening, or brazing.
3. **Forming** — Metal is bent into shape.
4. **Casting** — Solid metal is melted or pressed to turn into a powder and put into a mold to create a shape.

Additive manufacturing is a new type of manufacturing process. Most often referred to as 3D printing, a shape is created on a computer in three dimensions and downloaded into a machine. The machine uses the file to build the object by taking base material and very precisely depositing it as layers, a small amount at a time, into a three-dimensional shape. The material is commonly plastic, but the process has been expanding rapidly to include metals, epoxy, concrete, and even biological cells.

Outside of commercial manufacturing, ordinary people can create objects using a 3D printer. A handheld scanner can be used to create the image of an existing shape or 3D designs that have been created by others can be purchased and downloaded from the Internet. (Additive manufacturing is described more fully in Chapter 10.)

Discussion Topics

Many types of manufacturing industries operate within the United States and specific geographic regions have prominence in one or more of them

1. Identify the industries that are prevalent in your region.
2. List the products that these industries manufacture.
3. Describe the processes that are required to create these products.

Chapter 6:
INTERNET OF THINGS, INDUSTRIAL INTERNET OF THINGS, INDUSTRY 4.0 – I'M SO CONFUSED

"Internet of Things is transforming the everyday physical objects that surround us into an ecosystem of information that will enrich our lives. From refrigerators to parking spaces to houses, the Internet of Things is bringing more and more things into the digital fold every day, which will likely make the Internet of Things a multi-trillion dollar industry in the near future."

— *PricewaterhouseCoopers report*

For many years, I have traveled throughout North America to discuss smart manufacturing technologies with educators and public policy makers at the local and state level. These are the people who will design, instruct, and financially support the next generation of skilled professionals, known as the "makers" of the future. Many of these individuals are not immersed in manufacturing operations and don't have deep personal experiences with them. They tend to rely on information published in the general press or on social media

They rarely if ever read technical trade publications focused on manufacturing.

How IoT, IIoT, and Industry 4.0 are Related

There is a lot of confusion about the terminology of the Internet of Things (IoT), the Industrial Internet of Things (IIoT), and Industry 4.0. Sometimes you will also hear about the Smart Factory or digital workplace. I illustrate my own understanding of what makes sense about these terms in the graphic below.

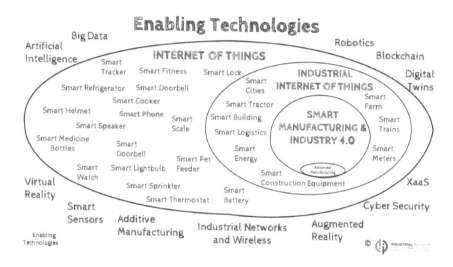

I title this diagram Enabling Technologies because these technologies are the individual bits that allow IoT, IIoT, and Smart Manufacturing to exist but do not constitute the IoT itself. I think of them as parts of the car — necessary for the vehicle but none are considered the automobile.

The IoT uses the enabling technologies in innovative ways to create consumer-grade devices, often called smart. These include smart speakers like Amazon's Echo or Google's Home, smart lightbulbs like Phillips' Hue, smart doorbell buttons like Arlo's video doorbell, and many others. These devices are used in homes and workplaces and make up a vast market.

The IIoT is a segment of the IoT. Smart cities, smart roads, smart trains, smart oilfields, and many others make up the IIoT. Devices developed for use in the IIoT monitor, alarm, or control industrial processes or specific equipment. Compared to more general, consumer-grade IoT products, IIoT devices need to be more physically robust and operate with a high degree of reliability.

Smart Manufacturing and Industry 4.0 are synonymous terms to me. They both focus on a sub-segment of the IIoT. Another term that is used interchangeably with these is advanced manufacturing but, in my view, that term specifically references only computer-controlled machine tools or CNC machines. As it represents only a small portion of all manufacturing, I have placed it as a bubble inside Industry 4.0.

The term Industry 4.0 reflects the idea that we now are experiencing the fourth industrial revolution in modern history.

The Four Industrial Revolutions

The first industrial revolution, the one we learned about in school, occurred in the 1800s and was precipitated by the steam engine's invention. Tasks previously carried out by human labor were transferred to machines. The result was enormously increased productivity in agriculture and textiles.

The second industrial revolution refers to the widespread use of electricity and the invention of Ford's assembly line, which created the mass production manufacturing model that continues to this day. It allowed the average person to own what had previously been luxuries only available to the rich. Again, productivity surged.

The third industrial revolution wasn't recognized as such until recently, though it actually started in 1969 with the invention of the programmable logic controller, or PLC. The PLC is a specialized computer used to control manufacturing processes. Introducing computer power into manufacturing created more efficient operations and surging production output. The third industrial revolution used computers to great advantage but for the most part, the computers operated individually and with few interconnections. The term "Islands of Automation" was coined to describe sophisticated work cells that had no automatic way to communicate with other parts of the company. There was simply no practical way of doing so.

The fourth industrial revolution, or Industry 4.0, refers to creating cyber-physical systems (CPS) that combine many different types of technologies together to develop a more sophisticated operation. The combination of these newly developed technologies into a coherent system enables a Digital Transformation of the enterprise. That means that data, in the form of digital information, is shared and acted upon automatically without human intervention. Recent advances in technology, which I discuss in several later chapters, provides data, computational power, and machine communications necessary for this to happen.

Industry 4.0 introduces the concept of *mass personalization* to replace the mass production paradigm. With Industry 4.0 technology, custom-designed products of the future will cost about the same as the mass-produced products of yesterday

You may be wondering, what makes Smart Manufacturing so exciting that I wrote a book about it? The reason is that it changes the mass production "push" manufacturing model into a *mass personalization* "pull" model. Up until now, manufacturers decided what they would make, pushing the product into the market in hopes that a customer would buy it. The customer had no input into the features of the product.

For example, if I am interested in buying a sport jacket, I go to a retail shop and try on several brands until I find one with a good enough color, good enough texture, and good enough fit to purchase. Usually, I can find something acceptable to buy. But I have to purchase what the *manufacturer* decided to sell. This is what happens today but not in the future.

In Smart Manufacturing, customers identify what they want in a product and pull that customized product from the manufacturer. So if I purchase a sport jacket from a Smart Manufacturer, I specify that I wish to purchase a 41-inch shoulder Donegal tweed jacket with 5% blue threads, 30.5-inch sleeves, and gray buttons. The smart manufacturer then produces it.

The consumer dictates the desired features and the manufacturer produces it to their specifications. This model is not different from the days before mass production when artisans created personalized products. There are still examples today such as going to a tailor, being measured, selecting the style and fabric, and receiving a single garment of exactly the color, texture, and fit wanted. The problem is that such personalization by an artisan can only be afforded by those with substantial means.

Smart Manufacturing provides a customized product at a mass-produced price. The impact of changing back to pull manufacturing is enormous and requires in-depth knowledge and skills — and a broad understanding of how everything needed for production fits together. Not that long ago, factory equipment performed one set function and modifying it for a customer request was not feasible. It is only recently that technology advanced to the level needed to make pull manufacturing possible.

I have friends who are engineers at a famous candy factory and years ago, they used to grumble about the holiday demands because their marketing department promised important customers personalized boxes of candy to sell. "Mike, the amount of time required to change over the machine takes the good part of a full day or more. During that time, we could have produced tens of thousands of boxes of candy. There is no way the specialized run of just a couple thousand boxes makes up for the loss." The company felt they had to take a loss with the specialized boxes of candy to keep the customer's business during the rest of the year. Today, equipment is more modular and flexible and so can meet customer demands more easily.

Smart manufacturers have three incentives driving the change toward mass personalization:

▸ First, they can seize sales and market share from slower-moving competitors that cannot provide customers with personalized products.

▸ Second, the technology used in pull manufacturing collects vast amounts of data needed for a predictive maintenance program. Predictive maintenance eliminates costs by reducing machine downtime caused by equipment failure and unnecessary preventive maintenance costs.

▸ Third, pull manufacturing involves an operations shift from made-to-stock to made-to-order. Instead of producing hundreds of jackets in every color, texture, and generic size possible, the smart manufacturer is only required to make one perfect jacket for a customer that has already promised to buy it and probably paid a deposit.

Pull manufacturing has a ripple effect in creating lower transportation costs, inventory reduction throughout the supply chain, and positive cash flow. This shift also reduces the enormous waste that is generated by mass production techniques in every industry.[9]

Over the last ten years, Amazon has provided a service that has increased expectations for more customization. You may wonder if the box of items you receive is unique and personal or at some time, someone else ordered the same items. In any case, mass-produced items fill your box, and the customization comes only from the supply chain consolidating them into one convenient package.

In Industry 4.0, when you order online, it is not supply chain equipment starting up but rather manufacturing equipment starting up to produce your unique product. Quite the exciting difference!

Discussion Topics

The Internet of Things technologies are strongly influencing the progression of manufacturing away from the mass production model towards a more individual customer-focused experience.

1. Which kinds of IoT devices would you like to see in the future?
2. Describe the similarities and differences between IIoT and IoT devices.
3. Identify two different industries or companies and describe the kinds of waste they produce. Discuss solutions to the waste problem.

Chapter 7:
WHAT XACTLY IS XAAS?

"While our customers' needs are met online by the people who do it better than anyone else, we will provide them with what we do best — the books, music and movies they love to explore in an engaging shopping atmosphere,"

— *Greg Josefowicz, Borders CEO, when outsourcing its online business to Amazon.*

It is conventional wisdom that every business — every successful business, at least — has a purpose. But in today's marketplace, it can be a mystery knowing exactly what business your business is in, even if you started the company. Common sales advice is to discuss outcomes, not features or benefits, to close a deal.

The idea is that no one really buys a drill, they buy a future hole. If some other technology came along, let's say a pocket laser that could make a hole faster or more cheaply, the manufacturers of traditional drills would lose sales. When this happens, it's rarely from market leaders. It's from industry outsiders.

Swiss watchmakers lost market share to Japanese electronics companies. Swedish and Norwegian cellphone manufacturers lost market share to Apple. Music labels and retailers lost market share to Internet music streaming services. Taxi companies lost market share to drivers participating in the gig economy. Nearly every brick-and-mortar retail store lost sales to online bookseller Amazon.

Over and over again, leading companies failed to pivot at the right time. They didn't fully realize what their businesses were, and entire markets were taken away by outsiders, as illustrated below by the losers in a hypothetical "Rock, Paper, Scissors" game:

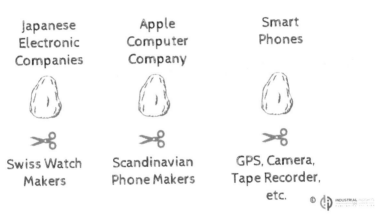

Outsiders Disrupt Entire Markets

Music companies defined their business as pressing or selling LP vinyl records. They thought so strongly that this was their business that they even tried to outlaw recordable cassette tape players. When Napster appeared, music companies not only sued the company but also the most loyal music customers the world has ever known. Napster had a centralized server so with enough foresight, someone could have purchased it and maybe attained what iTunes ultimately became.

The opening quote for this chapter was from a market leader, Borders bookstores, which thought their business was making pleasant retail environments to sell books. What they didn't recognize and so didn't prioritize was creating an e-reader and selling e-books and other paper books online. The leaders at Borders felt so strongly that creating a pleasant physical ambience was their business that they contracted with Amazon to distribute their books online. They failed to recognize that they were, indeed, in the book selling business and inviting a competitor to service their customers was misguided. Just ten years later, Borders went out of business.

Let me share a powerful idea. Most of the time, the thing being purchased is simply the means to a desired *outcome*. If a better means is developed, it will replace the previous version and the true business is revealed.

For example, when I buy a handheld drill, do I really want to have a five-pound device sitting in my basement unused for months at a time? My real need, and the business that the drill maker is in, is providing round holes of different diameters.

Suppose another technology is developed that creates holes better, faster, or cheaper than a handheld drill does? Maybe a cell phone sized device with a powerful laser. What do you think I'll purchase and what risks do the handheld drill companies face if they aren't also adopting and discovering better ways of making holes?

Everything as a Service?

This is where XaaS comes in: "Everything as a Service."

Software companies were the first to realize that customers wanted outcomes and packaged their offerings as services instead of products. Instead of buying a software package for hundreds, thousands, or even millions of dollars, they devised a new business model, called software as a service, or **SaaS**.

SaaS began with corporate software but soon became available for personal use. Home office suites now cost as little as $12 per month. Sellers love consistent income flows. Buyers love that small upgrades and security patches can be automated. The consequence is a rethinking of what a business is because whether equipment, tools, supplies, pressurized air, or aircraft engines, all can be offered as a service.

AaaS — Air as a Service? The company Kaeser Compressors will place air compressors in your factory and charge you by usage.

BaaS — Books as a Service? Pay a subscription and read as many Kindle or Nook books as you want.

IaaS — Ink as a Service? HP charges $4 per 100 printed pages per month. Print less and you receive a credit, print more and you pay more.

EaS — Engines as a Service? Rolls-Royce charges airlines per flying mile, not while the planes are on the ground getting service.

MaaS — Music as a Service? Pay a monthly fee and stream all the music you want on Spotify and other platforms.

RaaS — Robots as a Service? Several start-up robot companies provide automation to companies that don't want to make their own considerable investment.

XaaS — Everything as a Service? Maybe!

One other benefit of XaaS is that services often come with performance guarantees and so maintenance responsibility shifts to the supplier. Companies can concentrate on their core business. And, hopefully, they know what it is.

What does this have to do with Smart Manufacturing? XaaS enables companies to focus on their core business and even understand better what its core business is by thinking of a better answer to the question, "What am I actually selling?" For example, a water filter maker might include a sensor that notifies the user when it needs to be replaced and even automatically orders the filter as part of a contract. The customer wants clean water, not own the filter. In the next chapters, as I explore the technologies of Smart Manufacturing, I encourage you to think about how they could be used to provide a desired outcome.

Discussion Topics

Understanding how your business satisfies customer's needs is required in Smart Manufacturing, where products are increasingly being packaged as part of a service.

1. List a few XaaS businesses you patronize and explain why these services are worth the price you pay.
2. Identify two other products you currently buy that could become X as a service.
3. Do you believe there are any risks of XaaS and if so, what are these risks?

ENABLING TECHNOLOGIES: THE HARDWARE GADGETS AND GIZMOS

Chapter 8:
INDUSTRIAL NETWORKS AND CYBERSECURITY

"Despite continued security problems, the IoT will spread and people will become increasingly dependent on it. The cost of breaches will be viewed like the toll taken by car crashes, which have not persuaded very many people not to drive."

— *Richard Adler, Distinguished Fellow at Institute for the Future*

For those not familiar with a modern manufacturing plant, it may come as a surprise to learn that there are usually thousands, if not tens of thousands, of I/O points in the control systems that run the machines. The "I" stands for "Inputs" to the control system and consists of sensors of various sorts such as temperature, level, flow, pressure, presence, and vibration. The "O" stands for "Outputs" and consists of valve actuators, solenoid valves, motor starters, and other parts that each create an action.

Networks

Computer networks simply connect devices together with wires or radio signals. You are undoubtedly familiar with many types of networks including Ethernet, USB, Bluetooth, Wi-Fi, or ZigBee. (RFID is a special type of network and sensor combined, which I will discuss in Chapter 11.) Ethernet is the most popular because it was invented in the 1970s by Xerox and became the standard network used in offices worldwide to connect computers to printers, other computers, and storage disks. Wi-Fi is the wireless version of Ethernet. If you need to save data on your cellphone, you are likely to seek a connection to a Wi-Fi network.

Industrial Ethernet is widely used in manufacturing and is simply Ethernet that is "hardened" to resist the harsher environment on the plant floor, such as waterproof connectors. As it looks different than standard Ethernet, it has become its own specialization. If you are interested in knowing more, the link in the endnotes is to a presentation in which I explained the differences in detail.[10]

Wireless networks, using radio waves, provide flexibility and convenience. A common wireless network that almost everyone is aware of is Wi-Fi, which connects to smart phones and doesn't count towards the cellular data limits. There are many other versions of wireless networks currently in use in both consumer grade and industrial settings.

I was responsible for launching my company's first industrial wireless products in the early 2000s. One of the first applications was with the New York subway system. We had to do a site survey in one of the tunnels under the East River. When working in subway tunnels, you just don't go down into the tunnel because of the dangers. You first need to attend a four-hour safety class and pass an exam before being permitted to enter the tunnels. For example, when a train passes, you have to hold on tight to the side of the tunnel so you don't get sucked onto the track.

Subway lines are metal-encased tunnels. A small voltage from a battery room between stations prevents corrosion from forming and protects the metal from rust. Once a month, a maintenance technician had to go to each battery room to make the voltage measurement. Our solution was to transmit the value of the voltage signal via a radio to eliminate the need for this inspection by transmitting the information directly to the control room.

It worked well, except when a train came by. As trains take up nearly the whole tunnel, they blocked the radio signal. We got into a long discussion about how to prevent the signal from being blocked by installing additional equipment until someone realized that we were breaking a golden "business sense" rule. Previously, the technician recorded voltage levels once a month. Our system communicated it several thousand times every hour. It was a huge improvement and cost saver -- even if trains blocked the signal regularly.

The incident illustrated how easy it is to get caught up in technology and forget the original purpose. This can be an issue, especially when a group consists of only engineers and other technically oriented people who jump at the chance to fix a problem before exploring whether it's a problem at all.

My friend, Adam Livesay, co-founder of the innovative IIoT start-up Elevāt, said it best: "If you aren't solving a business problem, it's a science project." With Smart Manufacturing, it's all about the business results — and employing technology to get there.

The most cutting-edge wireless technology is the 5G network. It is the next generation of cellular networks and just being deployed today. Cellular networks are what your cell phone uses to make calls and download apps if you are not connected to Wi-Fi. The speed and extended bandwidth of 5G allows a high-definition video to stream on phones with no lag in the signal. Increased bandwidth makes the augmented and virtual applications that I will discuss in Chapter 13 more feasible for training and maintenance operations.

Cybersecurity in the Industrial Plant

Imagine a scenario in which terrorists use their knowledge of industrial control systems and operations technology to pulsate valves in an oil refinery, causing a massive explosion. Fortunately, to the best of my knowledge, this hasn't happened but it was the opening plot of the bestselling book *Red Storm Rising* by Tom Clancy that was published in 1983.

In 2010, the most famous real case of an industrial computer attack occurred. The Stuxnet computer worm infected 200,000 Iranian computers and 1000 sophisticated centrifuges, destroying that country's ability to refine uranium.[11] Stuxnet was extremely sophisticated and destroyed the infected equipment by creating intense vibrations by unbalancing the load. It was similar to the loud thumping you might hear if you put a large, soaking wet towel into a clothes dryer. In this case, the centrifuges were spinning uranium.

When Ethernet is discussed, security is right behind because its workings are well known to hackers. Industry cybersecurity is a fast-growing field that is likely to become more so in the future. I will discuss two areas that I believe deserve special attention. (Cybersecurity will also be discussed in Chapter 16 in the section on blockchain technologies.)

Security Concerns on the Plant Floor

As more devices are connected to a network, the "threat area" to hacking becomes greater. Connectivity is an excellent advantage for communication but access to only the right people at the right time must be ensured.

A manufacturing plant must be careful about any data that unintentionally leak out of the facility. The goal should be none. When aggregated over time, even tiny data points can yield surprising information about an organization. Furthermore, if data can exit, other threats such as trojans, viruses, and ransomware can enter.

Cybersecurity has become an essential function and those with cybersecurity expertise are in high demand. Network design and protection will remain a top job for the foreseeable future.

Security Concerns Inside a Smart Device

IIoT devices such as temperature and vibration sensors, controllers, and scales use ethernet chipsets to communicate on the Ethernet network, either wired or via Wi-Fi, and then often out to the Internet. Given these interactions through various networks, much care is needed when designing any smart device so that security isn't compromised. It is necessary for cybersecurity experts to work alongside device designers to ensure adherence to current security standards.

General Security Concerns

While hacker attacks are the most discussed cybersecurity threat, those in manufacturing must also be educated about simpler but effective attacks. Social engineering attacks pinpoint weaknesses in human nature to gain access to information.

The Stuxnet attack was reportedly launched via USB memory sticks given to workers at suppliers to the factory. Criminals have also used social media accounts to learn information about their victims before attacking them.

One day while at the office, a call came to me from someone claiming to be my company president wanting authorization for a wire transfer. I've been living in New Jersey for long enough to adapt its no-nonsense persona when needed. I hope his ear hurt when I slammed down the phone. But the scary part was that he knew the president's nickname and the company's reporting structure, so he could have been quite convincing to someone else.

On another occasion, I received an email that appeared to have been sent from our CEO's private Yahoo account. I was directed in the email to click a link of vital importance. As it didn't seem quite right, I immediately reported it to IT to perform the required defensive actions and warn others. As you may know, this type of email constitutes a phishing attack, which is a pun on the word fishing as the sender is fishing for information. Even if these types of attacks are successful only 0.001% of the time, the damage can be devastating.

Movies that Feature Cybersecurity

Even if you have little personal experience with issues of cybersecurity, you are likely to have encountered it in the media. For example, the following are just a few recent movies that incorporate cybersecurity into the story line.

TRON, Wargames, Hackers, Johnny Mnemonic, Sneakers, The Net, The Girl with the Dragon Tattoo, Untraceable, Inception, The Net,

Blackhat, Mission: Impossible — Ghost Protocol, Snowden, Zero Days (documentary about Stuxnet)

Examples of Careers in Industrial Control Systems and Cybersecurity

Positions that focus on the industrial control systems and cybersecurity are expected to grow in number and importance over the next decades, as factories become more automated and Smart Manufacturing becomes the standard manufacturing method.

Industrial Control System Network Security Engineer leads and innovates for network security solutions. This position works closely with internal and external resources to design, deploy, standardize, maintain, and audit the global network's industrial control systems. The positions typically require a college degree or demonstrated mastery of the subject. Salary range is currently $120–160k.

Industrial IoT Network Engineer leads technical resources and delivers industrial network services and solutions. This position works directly with customers to deliver assessments, designs, and implementations specific to industrial networks and virtualization solutions to leverage IIoT. Salary range is currently $87–110k.

IoT Embedded Engineer ensures that smart products designed by the smart manufacturer provide security at the embedded level (inside the device), cloud operations, and mobile platforms. Salary range is currently $120–150k.

Instrumentation and Control System Technician manages controls, calibration, and maintenance of the plant. Salary range is currently $60–80k.

Maintenance Technicians and Engineers maintain equipment when malfunctions are beyond the operator's ability. The job role is shifting towards more predictive actions that involve adjusting before failure and require understanding of many types of technology. These positions typically require a high school diploma plus some experience or certification. Salary range is currently $25-50K.

Discussion Topics

Central to all Smart Manufacturing operations is the use of computer networks to share information not only within the factory, but to suppliers and customers as well.

1. What could a hacker learn by capturing data from a manufacturing plant, such as energy usage?
2. Identify a few examples of everyday technologies that were hard-wired in the past and are now wireless.
3. Imagine that a manufacturer designs a smart IIoT device for its industrial customers and finds out later that there is a security problem. Discuss what should be done.

Chapter 9:
THE RISE OF THE ROBOTS

"We have to face the fact that countries are going to lose jobs to robotics. The only question that needs to be answered is which country will create and own the best robotic technology and have the infrastructure necessary to enable it."

— *Mark Cuban, Entrepreneur*

The Smart Factory promises to deliver customized products to customers at the same cost associated with mass production. Robots will play an expanded role in manufacturing as they free humans from machine-like jobs and duties, allowing them to concentrate on creative issues. However, robots are also one of the most feared technologies because many attribute job losses to automation, as shown in the opening quote. And yet nations that employ a large number of robots actually experience *fewer* job losses over time, contrary to what might seem to be common-sense wisdom.[12] The U.S. currently lags behind several countries in robot use but has recently begun to catch up.

Consider a job where heavy clay bricks need to be stacked onto a pallet for transportation to a job site or retail shop. It is hard, exhausting labor, and the numbers of available human brick stackers are limited to a few individuals with the physical power and aptitude to do such a job. Those without strength and stamina are unable to perform this job role.

Now consider a robotic system designed to stack bricks. The human needs to program the robot and ensure it is functioning correctly but doesn't have to lift the bricks. The number of people capable of performing the job increases tremendously. Removing physical strength as a prerequisite opens the door for more men and women to qualify. For example, someone who uses a wheelchair could be eligible for the brick stacking job! With remote communications, they may not even have to be in the same building.

Birgit Skarstein, a double paraplegic rowing athlete for Norway, stated it well:

"For people with a disability, the Fourth Industrial Revolution will give us super powers."

Let's look at the three exciting robot types used in manufacturing: industrial arms, mobile robots, and cobots.

Industrial Arms

Many robots deployed today have the function of mimicking a human arm with six axes of movement. They are useful in manufacturing processes where flexibility is needed because their action can be re-programmed at any time

The cost of robot arms has been decreasing and so their adoption rates have been increasing. Return on investment (ROI) studies are used to determine when an investment cost will be recouped. Lower prices for robots mean a higher ROI and, thus, investing in robots is more financially favorable than even a few years ago.

Mobile Robots

Automated Guided Vehicles (AGV) are already used in supply chain and manufacturing logistics operations to move products toward either the end customer or a value-add manufacturing process. Most designs require a pre-defined path that the AGV follows. This works well when nothing changes but isn't as flexible and agile as needed for the Smart Factory.

Mobile robots, on the other hand, can determine their path. If told that Part A needs to go to location B, it will figure out the exact way on its own. Or suppose Part A needs to go to location C the next day. No problem. The onboard computers consult a map of the workspace. The scanners then detect unexpected obstacles, including people, that can get in the way of the robot. The result is that the mobile robot will find an alternative route.

Mobile robots are essential in the supply chain. Amazon uses more than 100,000 and even purchased its own robotics company several years ago to ensure access to cutting-edge technology.[13]

Collaborative Robots (or Cobots)

Traditional robots are useful because they are fast and powerful as their motion comes from electrical motors. Anyone who has ridden in a Tesla has experienced firsthand how much low-end torque electric motors produce, accelerating from rest very rapidly.

This power also makes robots dangerous, so they must operate within enclosed cells, away from people. The first known death of a human by a robotic system was caused by a one-ton robot in 1979.[14]

The most common way of keeping humans safe is to keep robots behind a secured wire fence when the robot is operating. This requires planning, effort, time, and materials. However, the industry clearly needed a safe system that allows humans and robots to work together in the same physical space. Such a system would enable robots to perform repetitive tasks and humans to make the adaptations needed for flexible manufacturing.

New robots are called collaborative robots because they collaborate with humans to perform a task. A new word, cobot, was coined to cleverly describe these types of robots.

Cobots limit the speed and force the robots can apply, making them inherently safer. They can be very light, weighing just a few pounds, and can be made of softer material that is less likely to harm a person if it accidentally hits them. A cobot arm can be moved manually by just a few pounds of force, even when it's off the robot (typical robot arms will lock in place). Sensors inside robots detect if they touch an object or person and instantly stop the robot.

Even with cobots, safety concerns and risk assessment are still necessary. But in general, cobots require less physical caging and allow more direct robot-human interaction.

Also, cobot programming languages are new, very advanced, and developed to be as intuitive as possible to significantly reduce the programmer's learning curve. There are even ways to eliminate programming by guiding a cobot manually through a task and recording the motion. I have witnessed firsthand as teenagers programmed a robot to do a simple job in as little as twenty minutes. That is a game-changer for sure and the reason that many companies have entered the cobot industry.

Movies that Feature Robotics

The following are just a few recent movies that incorporates robotics into the story line sometimes as a villain out to kill a person or destroy all of humanity or as a more sympatric entity that causes us to ponder what makes something an intelligent or conscience being:

Ghost in the Shell, *Terminator*, *Metropolis* (made in 1927!), *Wall-E*, *RoboCop*, *The Iron Giant*, *I, Robot*

Careers in Robotics

There are a considerable variety of career opportunities for those interested in robotics within retail, food service, health care, and other industries. Although first used in manufacturing, the technology is finding applications in every industry.

Robot Operations Engineer is involved in hardware set up, troubleshooting, and sensor tuning for a fleet of robots. The position usually requires a college degree plus experience with robots. Salary range is currently $90–130k.

Robotics Engineer is involved in system integration, hands-on building, and custom automation cells. The position requires a minimum of three years of experience. Salary range is currently $70–130k.

Robot Field Service Technician is involved in programming and troubleshooting hardware and software, and solving and repairing issues at customer sites. The position typically requires an associate's degree or higher plus two years of experience and company training. Salary range is currently $65–75k.

Mechatronics Engineer is involved in setting up and troubleshooting robots and mechanical systems. The position requires broad knowledge and typically an associate's degree or high school diploma plus on-the-job training. Salary range is currently $50–100k.

Machine and Process Operators ensure that processes and equipment are producing products in the quantity and quality required. The job role is shifting from manually pushing buttons or loading and unloading material to using information technology to anticipate issues before they arise. These positions usually require a high school diploma and the ability to obtain various licenses to operate forklifts and other equipment, although exceptions are made. Salary range is currently $25-45K plus overtime.

Discussion Topics

Robotics are one of the most visible and discussed technologies used by Smart Manufacturing to increase the productivity and quality of production, and their use is projected to increase greatly in the foreseeable future.

1. Discuss the advantages that robots have over humans and the types of tasks they do best.
2. Discuss the advantages humans have over robots and how cobots might help perform tasks that robots can't do well enough.

Chapter 10:
A LITTLE BIT HERE, A LITTLE BIT THERE: ADDITIVE MANUFACTURING MATURES

"Manufacturing will shift from centralized factories to a distributed, domestic manufacturing future, thanks to the rise of 3D printer technology."

> — *Craig Venter, Founder of The Institute for Genomic Research*

I love to watch the old *Star Trek* episodes, with all the phasers, transport beams, and cool uniforms. The replicator was the device that could create anything you wanted — dinner, drinks, and spare parts for machinery.

It seems to me that additive manufacturing, sometimes referred to as 3D printing, is our replicator. It has probably done more to re-ignite our collective joy in building things than anything else in recent years. This rapidly advancing and evolving technology promises to revolutionize the act of making things among "real" manufacturers.

There are three main philosophies of making things: subtractive, formative, and additive. It's useful to compare the three to understand the processes.

Subtractive vs. Formative vs. Additive Manufacturing

Subtractive manufacturing starts with a block of something and by selectively removing material, the final product emerges. A sculptor chiseling a hunk of marble to form a beautiful statue is an example in the world of art. In manufacturing, consider the example of a worker or machine cutting, drilling, shaping, and polishing a metal item from a block or sheet of metal.

Formative manufacturing shapes raw material into its final form. A pottery maker spinning wet clay into a bowl is an example in the world of crafting. In manufacturing, an example is injection molding machines that may form plastic into bottles or toy farm animals.

Additive manufacturing builds layers of material to create an object. For centuries, this technique has been used by painters who build up layers of pigment to create their artwork. In manufacturing, machines are used for depositing tiny bits of material to grow an object.

Within the last decade, the equipment and controls needed to precisely deposit materials have advanced in capability and plummeted in pricing. The base materials have expanded from just nylon plastic to many types of powdered metals and other materials.

Around the year 2005, I worked for a company that used one of the most advanced 3D printers to make prototype parts of a type of electrical connector. The results were fragile and nonfunctional. But compared to either hand-making a clay model or showing 2D drawings, it was a significant improvement. Just ten years later, smaller and more capable machines became available at office supply stores for a fraction of the price. These have intuitive user interfaces for non-technologists and the finished product is as functional as the design enables. In Smart Manufacturing, 3D printing produces real parts, not just prototypes. The image below shows the most common types of 3D printing:

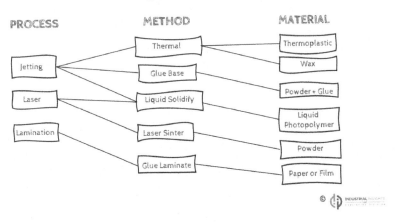

Described below are the seven main types of additive manufacturing, with the endnote directing you to a website with illustrations of how each one functions:[15]

Photopolymerization transforms a liquid polymer within a vat into a solid using an ultraviolet light beam that hardens the liquid into a solid only where the light hits it.

Material jetting sprays a liquid polymer onto a surface and an ultraviolet light beam hardens it. More and more layers are deposited, creating the end product.

Binder jetting uses a glue-like material to bond powered materials together, layer after layer.

Material extrusion feeds a plastic filament, similar to nylon fishing string, through a heated nozzle to melt, then deposits it in thin layers.

Powder Bed Fusion fuses a bed of powder with a laser or electron beam to form a solid part, layer by layer.

Sheet Lamination cuts thin layers of foil or paper into layers either by laser or mechanically. These are then fused with ultrasonic welding to form an object.

Direct Energy Deposition melts metal powders or wires and creates a workpiece layer by layer.

Let me also mention that additive manufacturing can create objects that would be nearly impossible with other methods. If you search online, you will find complex and interesting 3D printed parts, and the list grows daily!

In 2015, I attended an engineering conference hosted by the U.S. National Academy of Engineering in Washington, D.C., where leaders in the aviation industry discussed new technologies to improve operations. They discussed how aircraft represent a considerable capital equipment investment for an airline. The only time airlines generate revenue is when they are carrying paying customers. The cost of not flying is estimated to be $150,000 per day for a Boeing 747 Max.[16]

When an aircraft part needs replacement and the plane is not allowed to fly, the result is downtime during which no revenue is generated. If the plane is in a remote location, it could take several weeks to receive a replacement part. The conference attendees considered a better way. One engineering executive from a well-known aerospace manufacturer in Washington State noted that his company was purchasing 40,000 3D printers to deploy in far-flung airports worldwide. Need a part? Download and print it locally.

The size of components that can be 3D printed has also increased substantially. One startup company has designed a system to 3D print full-size, functional rocket engines. It uses robotics to perform the precise movements required and artificial intelligence to improve quality control.[17]

In regulated industries like aerospace, stringent rules apply to confirm that all purchased items are genuine because counterfeiting is a present danger and serious risk to safety. This regulatory requirement doesn't disappear with additive manufacturing. Blockchain assures the airline that the downloaded file is what it says it is and that the seller is who they say they are. (I discuss blockchain in more detail in Chapter 16.)

Finally, this chapter primarily focused on business-to-business (B2B) applications of additive manufacturing. However, business-to-consumer (B2C) business opportunities are just as exciting as people reimagine what is possible. I will leave you with the following quote from a famous fashion designer:

"Forget shopping, soon we will be able to download our clothes."

— *Danit Peleg, Fashion Designer known for 3D printed clothing*

Movies that Feature Additive Manufacturing

The following are just a few recent movies that incorporates some form of 3D printing or additive manufacturing into the story line and generally show the advantage of being able to make anything you need exactly when you need it:

Any Star Trek film, The Fifth Element, Jurassic Park III, Mission: Impossible III, Ocean's 8, The Cloverfield Paradox, Hotel Artemis, Black Panther, and *Print the Legend* (a documentary about 3D printing)

Careers in Additive Manufacturing

What job positions involve additive manufacturing? Creative positions are involved in creating products that take advantage of the capabilities of additive manufacturing while more technical positions are involved with designing and maintaining the equipment.

Production Technician is responsible for running the machinery and material handling devices. The position typically requires a high school diploma plus the ability to pass tests on basic skills. Typical salary is currently $25-40k.

Additive Manufacturing Engineer works with customers to design solutions for their needs. The position typically requires an engineering degree. Salary range is currently $77–110k.

Product Designer creates products for manufacturing with 3D printers and other methods. The position typically requires an engineering or related degree. Salary range is currently $55–75k.

Traditional manufacturing jobs include welding, joining, assembly, and pipe fitting but with automation, the job is shifting to managing that automation. These positions require a high school diploma or GED plus some experience or certification. Salary range is currently $25-50K plus overtime.

Discussion Topics

3D printing has rapidly progressed from large devices costing hundreds of thousands of dollars to hobbyist models available for less than $200 sold in office supply stores, bringing the technology to everyone.

1. What are current limitations of additive manufacturing?
2. How can 3D printing reduce costs for a company?
3. How might additive manufacturing techniques be used in industries such as construction and health care?

Chapter 11:
SENSOR PRICES ARE FALLING DOWN, FALLING DOWN, FALLING DOWN

"When we talk about the Internet of Things, it's not just putting RFID tags on some dumb thing so we smart people know where that dumb thing is. It's about embedding intelligence, so things become smarter and do more than they were proposed to do."

— *Nicholas Negroponte, Founder of MIT's Media Lab*

One of the foundational technologies of Industry 4.0 is smart sensors. These sensors measure physical parameters such as temperature, vibration, humidity, electrical power, presence, acceleration, and liquid and gas concentrations. They provide that data on the process, equipment, or environment.

Many sensors act as fancy switches, simply letting you or a piece of equipment know if something has occurred. They have recently become plentiful, sophisticated, and inexpensive. It is hard to comprehend how Industry 4.0 could exist without the data that sensors provide.

Though integral to manufacturing, sensors also exist in your house. The following are just a few examples:

▸ Open the fridge door and the light comes on.

▸ Open the microwave when its running and it shuts off.

▸ Start the dishwasher and water runs until hot water comes from the pipes.

▸ Close the garage door and it stops if someone walks under it while in motion.

▸ Back up in your driveway and the car will make a noise if someone or something is passing behind.

In manufacturing, sensors are the "Inputs" to the control system. An example might be that a sensor tells the controller that the "workpiece is in the correct position" to permit an operation like drilling a hole in it may occur.

I worked for one of the world's most innovative sensor companies in the 1990s. Sensors in 1995 sold for the equivalent of $350 in 2020 dollars. We sold competing electronic versions that required no physical touch. For example, your finger could come within 1mm of a doorbell button and without touching it, the doorbell would still ring. These were more reliable than mechanical sensors because they never wore out — no-touch means no wear.

In October 2020, those sensors are selling for about $50 with off-brands priced as low as $8. As the price drops, more applications become economically viable.

Another sensor technology, which was never widely considered a sensor until recently, is the imaging chip used in digital cameras. Both consumer and industrial cameras use these chips and they are fully electronic. IoT sensors followed a similar price curve; what cost $22 in 1992 sold for less than $1.50 in 2014.[18]

Along with the price reduction of all types of sensors has come an explosion of new applications. So let's take a deeper look at the features of today's sensors.

Wireless Communication Ability

Communicating data without connecting wires to the sensor offers cost and convenience benefits and is an essential aspect of the IIoT. These systems use Wi-Fi or a special industrial wireless system to transmit sensor data to other parts of the control system.

An essential wireless class is RFID, radio-frequency identification, which could be thought of as a memory stick that will transmit its information if asked. This technology has many uses, including anti-theft tags at retail shops and in automobile toll tag systems. As discussed earlier, each product is unique and customized in Smart Manufacturing. An RFID chip can be attached to a specific product, allowing information about it to be stored and updated during every part of the manufacturing process. The product can contain a complete history of itself and tell the machine what operations it requires.

Many RFID chips require no local power source. There is enough energy from the scanning device to "wake up" the sensor and transmit its information. This leads to the next topic, energy efficiency.

Energy Efficient

As sensors become smaller and cheaper, they require less power. Lower power requirements mean that no signal or power wires are needed and the sensors can be truly wireless.

When I had a product manager role, my team launched the first wireless product for my company, but it still needed power connections. The joke was always, "If it's wireless, why do we have to plug it in?"

Truly wireless sensors use solar or battery power without the need to connect to the grid. Some innovative designs can convert small vibrations into electricity to power the sensor indefinitely. Think of all the remote locations or hard-to-reach areas that would benefit from such technology.

Networkable

While wireless has opened up a huge market for smart sensor applications, wired networks still have an essential role. Smart sensors interface to Profibus DP, Ethernet/IP, IO-Link Foundation Fieldbus, HART, and Profinet PA networks. You may not be familiar with those names but many are forms of Industrial Ethernet (described in Chapter 8) and allow devices to communicate with each other.

Smart

You may still be wondering, what is a smart sensor? It is a sensor that can not only sense a specific condition but can perform an action based upon what it experiences. A smart sensor may start transmitting data only when it detects conditions crossing an alarm threshold. By communicating only important information, power is conserved and the amount of data that the network must transmit is reduced.

Smart sensors are used in the manufacturing process to convey information about the manufacturing process or the health of equipment, which is sometimes referred to as condition monitoring. One example is an oil quality sensor that keeps track of the deterioration of the fluid and informs the maintenance staff when it's time to change the fluid. Another application is the use of a sensor that monitors the power that a pump motor is consuming. As the power level increases, it might authorize a second pump to start so the first isn't overloaded

Monitoring

Smart sensors can be attached to existing equipment to make the equipment's condition, or health, more visible. Currently, most facilities use a preventive maintenance strategy, which means that maintenance operations take place after a preset amount of time. This is like being notified by a light in your automobile to change the oil because it was last changed 5000 miles or six months previously.

Preventative maintenance is a good strategy for keeping equipment running but it is also very expensive because maintenance is often performed before it is really needed. There is also the possibility that when performing the maintenance, something else might break unexpectedly, causing yet further expense.

Smart sensors are a key component of implementing a different strategy called predictive maintenance. When using this strategy, maintenance is implemented only as absolutely required and based upon pertinent data. In the automobile example, a car with an oil quality sensor only alerts the driver when the oil requires replacement. It could be 10,000 miles or 1,000 miles, but only when required.

Alarm, Control, and Prediction

A sensor with enough computing power might be able to do more than just monitor and alarm. It might even be able to perform corrective action. For example, if a high-end freezer contains a redundant compressor unit, the sensor could direct the shutdown of the faulty one and start up the spare, which would be invaluable for a meat packing and selling facility. Perhaps it could even predict the failure by monitoring key variables, such as the vibration of the motor. Most of this is currently performed outside the sensor today but if trends continue, this functionality is likely to be incorporated directly into the sensor in the near future.

Sensors provide information about the physical world, the state of the manufacturing process, and the equipment's condition. Digital twins (discussed in Chapter 15) use the data to create hyper-realistic models of the equipment in which the sensors are used, which open up whole new areas of opportunity for a Smart Factory.

Movies that Feature Smart Sensors

Of course, many science fiction movies incorporate various sensors into the plot line as do many bank heist movies where the characters must avoid or outsmart the sensors to avoid getting caught. Some notable films are:

Mission Impossible, Ocean's Eleven, Total Recall, Bladerunner, Smart House

Careers in Sensors

Most positions in sensors require a bachelor's degree or higher in engineering, computer science, or related discipline. Jobs exist at companies that create and manufacture new types of sensors as well as the companies that use them as part of a larger system.

Mechatronics Engineer integrates new sensors like cameras, lidar, and radar into autonomous platforms of a working system. Typical salary is currently $75–110k.

Sensor Product Engineer develops and maintain software platforms. Typical salary is currently $82–110k.

Sales and Application Engineer finds solutions to the problems and needs of the individual customer. Typical salary is currently $70-$90 plus commission.

Product Marketing Manager provides product support to sales using design sales tools such as brochures, presentations, and online content that position the company as a leader in the field. Typical salary is currently $75-$115k.

Discussion Topics

Smart manufacturing requires collecting and acting upon information that is often produced by sensors deployed throughout the factory

1. What types sensors might be used in a machine that is making paper?
2. Research the types of sensors used in a smartphone and their possible manufacturing applications.
3. What is Moore's Law and how does it apply to sensor technology?

SECTION V:
ENABLING TECHNOLOGIES: STODGY SOFTWARE AND COOL APPS

Chapter 12:
BIG DATA AND VISUALIZATION
OF INFORMATION

"Big Data will spell the death of customer segmentation and force the marketer to understand each customer as an individual within 18 months or risk being left in the dust."

— *Ginni Rometty, former Executive Chair and CEO of IBM*

Smart Manufacturing requires smart devices, and all those smart devices generate a huge amount of data. It turns out that generating colossal data sets is a lot easier than interpreting them! Key performance indicators, or KPIs, are bits of data that collate directly to a process, factory, or company's performance. KPIs are dependent on company goals. For example, if good customer service is essential, tracking on-time delivery percentages would be an important KPI. For industries that need their plants to produce the maximum amount of products every day, equipment availability would be a critical KPI.

The Five "V"s of Big Data

It used to be that relevant data were hard to obtain. But with smart sensors and devices, this is no longer true as they generate big data sets that challenge human comprehension because of the volume, variety, velocity, visibility, or value of the data.

▸ **Volume** refers to the amount of data produced, usually the number of bits of information. Not only is the volume of data growing rapidly but the rate of growth is also increasing.

▸ **Variety** refers to the types of data collected. For structured data, labels are attached to each data point so it is clear what the data represent. A chart of the high and low temperatures for every day in November of a certain year would be an example. Unstructured data are much harder to define. For example the number of times the word "hot" occurred in Twitter posts in the same month could be referring to many things depending on the context of the tweet.

▸ **Velocity** refers to the speed of the data generation and how often it is updated. This is important because older information may no longer be useful. For example, if you made a decision to turn on the air conditioner based only on the previous day's high temperature, you might find yourself feeling much too cold because the outside temperature had dropped in 24 hours.

▸ **Visibility** means seeing information elsewhere in the company through software systems called SCADA, MES, or ERP platforms discussed in Chapter 17. Throughout the entire enterprise, information is visible on graphical dashboard displays from "shop floor to top floor." Various dashboards are used so often that it can become highly confusing, as shown in the humorous graphic below:

▸ **Value** refers to how effectively an organization can turn data into information and increase wealth generation. Value answers the "why" question when it comes to big data.

Common Dashboard Screens

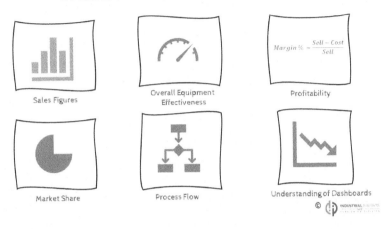

Sales Figures

Overall Equipment Effectiveness

Profitability

Market Share

Process Flow

Understanding of Dashboards

Finally, there are many discussions about the source of big data and where it resides. If you are interested in exploring more about big data, I suggest you research cloud, fog, and edge data and computing.

Movies that Feature Data and Big Data

The following are just a few recent movies that incorporate data or big data into the story line, where deeper understanding of information is used to make a better decision or outcome:

Moneyball is based on a true story about how big data was used to recruit baseball players to the Oakland A's team. *21* used data to win card games. *Minority Report* used data for crime prevention.

Careers in Big Data[19]

Most positions in big data require a university degree and some require an advanced degree in computer science, data science, applied mathematics, or similar program.

Data Analyst determines trends in data. Typical salary is currently $75–100k.

Data Engineering Specialist is involved in architecting and delivering highly scalable, high-performance data integration and transformation platforms. The solutions the data engineering specialist seeks include cloud, hybrid, and legacy environments requiring breadth and depth of data engineering skills. Typical salary is currently $100–140k.

Data Architect designs IT systems to collect, display, and analyze data. Typical salary is currently $110–150k.

Discussion Topics

The amount of data being produced every second within a Smart Manufacturing plant is beyond the ability of humans to act upon, so software systems that can help understand what the data means will continue to be a sought-after expertise

1. What traditional types of data would a manufacturer find useful?
2. How could a manufacturer leverage social media big data?
3. How could a manufacturer use big data to analyze its supply chain?

Chapter 13:
SKIP THE DRUGS, ALTERNATIVE REALITIES ARE ALREADY HERE

"As the Internet of Things advances, the very notion of a clear dividing line between reality and virtual reality becomes blurred, sometimes in creative ways."

— *Geoff Mulgan, Professor at University College London*

Two of the flashier software developments are augmented and virtual reality systems. Both technologies offer manufacturers with improved capabilities to provide training to their employees, model prototypes of equipment, and learn better ways to operate equipment or facilities. For example, Microsoft Xbox controller or HaloLens developed by the video gaming industry have had industrial applications in graphic engines and interfaces.

Augmented Reality

According to Merriam-Webster, augmented reality is an "enhanced version of reality created by the use of technology to overlay digital information on an image of something being viewed through a device (such as a smartphone camera)."

In the consumer world, augmented reality apps are available from a variety of sellers. Want to see how your house looks with a new paint color? There's an app! How would that modern sofa look in your family room? There's an app! What's the backstory about this bottle of wine? There's an app!

To use augmented reality, an app is installed on a smartphone or tablet that then uses its camera to detect either a standard object (like a table) or a special object (like a QR code). Each app is designed to recognize certain images depending on what its use is, and when it detects the object, it provides additional information over the image that is displayed on the screen.

In this way, the physical world depicted on the screen is augmented, or made greater, by additional visual overlays. If the app is designed for a retail store, when it detects the table, it might place a virtual vase on top of it. I recently downloaded an app from a paint store and when it recognized room walls, I was able to simulate a new paint color on them.

One early use of augmented reality in manufacturing was to provide faster and easier industrial maintenance operations. This simplest operation involved looking for a piece of equipment with a QR code on it. When found, additional information might pop up on the screen, such as a written troubleshooting guide.

Consider working in a plant and being asked to get a machine up and running. The number of devices and components is overwhelming — especially if you have to go back to the documentation room to look up information and then go back out to the floor again.

This is where augmented reality makes a difference; all that information, from lists of parts and troubleshooting guides to schematic diagrams and installation manuals, are available. Some commercially available systems provide a type of X-ray that serves as a picture of the equipment, allowing workers to see what is hidden from view.

Since many manufacturers measure downtime at $1000 per minute or even much more, the savings in quickly fixing equipment by using augmented reality is significant.

How about cases for which the published written material and drawings aren't sufficient to solve the problem? Perhaps a real-time discussion with an expert, even the person who built the device, would be helpful. Advances in augmented reality systems are making this a possibility.

Apart from maintenance, augmented reality has replaced paper and static screen systems for other applications such as assembly tasks, equipment training, and safety training.

Virtual Reality

According to Merriam-Webster, virtual reality is "an artificial environment which is experienced through sensory stimuli (such as sights and sounds) provided by a computer and in which one's actions partially determine what happens in the environment."

Virtual reality is both more impressive and more cumbersome than augmented reality because it requires a full headset that immerses the user's perceptions into the cyber world along with several external cameras to capture movements and the physical environment in 3D rendering. At present, some of the more prominent names in virtual reality headsets include Oculus Rift, LG, Sony Playstation VR, HTC Vive, Microsoft HoloLens, and Samsung Gear VR.

Some early applications for virtual reality in Smart Manufacturing include intensive training on new skills and orientation training for new employees. Virtual reality protects expensive equipment and provides a safe way to train the employees. At Ford Motor Company, a virtual reality setup with a twenty-three camera motion-capture system immerses the employee in a virtual replica of a real workstation. Additionally, another system uses fifty-two cameras to capture worker movements that are analyzed to improve safety, resulting in a 70% reduction in injuries.[20]

Movies that Feature Augmented and Virtual Reality

The following are just a few recent movies and tv series that incorporate augmented and virtual reality into the story line, most of which belong to the science fiction or action genre:

TRON, They Live, Minority Report, Iron Man, Terminator 2: Judgment Day, Back to the Future Part II, Total Recall, Inception, Blade Runner 2049, The Matrix, Upload (Netflix TV series), *Black Mirror* ("San Junipero" episode of the Netflix TV series)

Careers in Augmented and Virtual Reality[21]

These positions usually require a degree in computer science, gaming, or engineering related to electronic devices and displays. They represent another rapidly growing field of technology and will be in demand for the foreseeable future

Software Developer develops immersive reality features into products. Typical salary is currently $82–110k.

Virtual Reality/Augmented Reality Developer creates learning and support systems. Salary is currently $80–100k.

Product and Project Managers lead product and project designs by working with many different organizational teams. Typical salary is currently $75-$110k

Discussion Topics

Augmented and virtual reality systems are being incorporated in nearly every industry including Smart Manufacturing.

1. How could they be used for training a new employee?
2. How could augmented and virtual reality assist in customer sales?
3. What engineering uses might benefit from augmented reality and virtual reality technologies?

Chapter 14:
ARTIFICIAL INTELLIGENCES BEGIN THEIR ASCENT

"Whenever I hear people saying AI is going to hurt people in the future I think, yeah, technology can generally always be used for good and bad and you need to be careful about how you build it ... if you're arguing against AI then you're arguing against safer cars that aren't going to have accidents, and you're arguing against being able to better diagnose people when they're sick."

— *Mark Zuckerberg, CEO and Co-founder of Facebook*

Artificial intelligence and robotics probably capture the most anticipation and fear regarding the automated future. What is clear is that artificial intelligence, often referred to as AI for short, is advancing rapidly in many different industries.

So, what is artificial intelligence? According to Andrew Moore, a former dean at Carnegie Mellon University, "Artificial intelligence is the science and engineering of making computers behave in ways that, until recently, we thought required human intelligence."[22]

Other Names for Artificial Intelligence

Artificial intelligence has a public relations image problem in that it doesn't get any respect, or, more accurately, credit for its achievements. As soon as the technology becomes commonplace, the AI label is dropped and is only used to describe future capabilities, not present achievements, as shown in the graphic below.

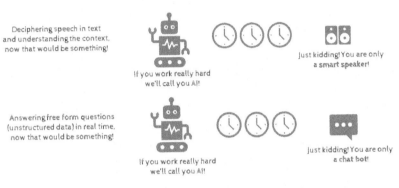

Consider the following accomplishments of artificial intelligence:

▸ **Voice recognition:** It's easy to forget how greatly voice recognition has advanced. In the late 1980s, one of my undergraduate classmates pursuing an electronics engineering and computer science double major struggled to have a single word understood by the computer in the senior project. This guy was brilliant and is now a professor of computer science at a well-known east coast university. Today, every handheld device has this capability because of advances in AI technology.

▸ **Social media feeds:** These feeds learn from your interactions and personalize the experience by suggesting new friends, advertising products, and more.

▸ **Facial recognition:** Like voice recognition, it has advanced to be almost omnipresent and increasingly more accurate. Facial recognition is used for various security and identification purposes.

▸ **Siri, Alexa, and other voice assistants:** These devices not only recognize speech but interpret it to provide information back to the speaker, all within seconds.

▸ **Smart maps:** Google, Waze, and others calculate the best routes and alternatives in real-time based on information such as maps and input from other users.

▸ **Movie recommendations:** Streaming channels capture everything you watch on their platforms and use this information to suggest other content that you might enjoy. So if you watch the movies listed at the end of each chapter of this book, you will find that the list of recommended films that your streaming service suggests will change.

Newsworthy artificial intelligence achievements in history include the following:

▸ In 1994, the University of Alberta's Chinook computer defeated the world-class human checker players.

▸ In 1996, IBM's Deep Blue defeated world chess champion Garry Kasparov.

▸ In 2011, IBM's Watson computer defeated two previous human champions on the game show *Jeopardy*. That same year, Apple introduced Siri.

▸ In 2016, Google's DeepMind AlphaGo defeated world Go champion Lee Sedol.

A computer defeated the top human chess player for the first time in 1996. The last time a human to beat the top computer was in 2005, showing just how fast the technology is improving.

Today, nearly 30% of artificial intelligence manufacturing applications are involved in maintaining machinery and other production assets. The other most frequent applications involve product quality inspection and demand planning, such as the following:

▶ Cameras to spot signals that robot components are failing at an automotive plant.

▶ Software to optimize additive manufacturing product design in order to use less material.

▶ Cameras or x-ray that detect defective parts.

While it may have previously been someone's job to do a repetitive task, it is now someone else's job to program, deploy, and maintain those robots, which enable them to earn a higher level of compensation than the previous job paid. Artificial intelligence frees human workers from doing routine tasks that can be draining and prevent them from being creative.

Moravec's paradox states that it is easy to train computers to do things that humans find hard, such as mathematics and logic, but it is hard to train them to do things humans find easy, like walking, image recognition, and being cool. The image from xkcd comics below illustrates the paradox.[23]:

Artificial intelligence enables humans to exert their creativity rather than carry out tasks, such as crunching numbers.

Machine learning is a related concept. Sometimes abbreviated as ML, machine learning involves the capability of a system to automatically learn and improve performance based on experience without the need for additional programming. Machine learning systems are trained rather than programmed to recognize certain phenomena.

For example, if a specific machine learning program aims to identify vegetables in photographs, thousands of pictures are scanned to provide enough information to confirm the answer regardless of the differences in appearance and context of the vegetable. After learning what specific vegetables, such as carrots, look like in many photos, the machine learning program is able to identify carrots in new images. Machine learning is the workforce of today's artificial intelligence.

There are currently three main types of learning methods used to create artificial intelligence systems:

▶ **Supervised learning:** The machine is told what patterns to detect. An example is when your streaming media device suggests a movie based on your viewing history.

▶ **Unsupervised learning:** The machine analyzes raw data, often unstructured data or data without labels, to determine anomalies. According to an article in 2018 in the *MIT Technology Review*, unsupervised learning is not as popular as supervised learning and is used primarily in cybersecurity and other similar applications.

▶ **Reinforcement learning:** Given an objective, the machine uses a Darwinian trial-and-error approach to problem solving. It is allegedly used in the AlphaGo program mentioned earlier.

Movies that Feature Artificial Intelligence

The following are just a few recent movies that incorporate artificial intelligence into the story line often causing the viewer to ponder how powerful technology might go terribly wrong:

Her, Ex Machina, Bladerunner 2049, 2001: A Space Odyssey, Ghost in the Shell, War Games

Careers in Software and Artificial Intelligence[24]

These careers typically require a degree in computer science or related area, and a master's degree or higher is sometimes required. Manufacturers are competing with every other industry to bring in talent that can work with and develop AI systems.

Embedded Systems Software Engineer provides code in electronic devices to communicate with AI systems. Typical salary is currently $85–110k.

Machine Learning Specialist designs and develops computer algorithms that have the ability to learn from data and make predictions about future situations. Typical salary is currently $110–$140k.

Robotics Engineer (for **Machine Learning and Artificial Intelligence**) develops algorithms, artificial intelligence, and machine-learning capabilities for innovative manufacturing processes and automation tools. Typical salary is currently $110–150k.

Data Scientist evaluates and uses algorithms for natural language processing (NLP), artificial intelligence, and machine learning applications. Typical salary is currently $130–160k.

Artificial Intelligence Engineer (for **Human Factors**) develops human-like autonomy that can learn behaviors from a small number of video demonstrations by actors. Typical salary is currently $100–150k.

Discussion Topics

Artificial intelligence is already eliminating the human element in performing repetitive mental tasks but there are differing views on how quickly this technology should be developed.

1. Research and discuss the views of three prominent people who consider artificial intelligence extremely dangerous and believe it needs to be controlled.

2. Research and discuss the views of three prominent people who think that artificial intelligence will improve human lives immensely.

3. Share other examples of artificial intelligence in medicine or healthcare, finance, or other industry.

Chapter 15:
DIGITAL TWINS MIRROR REALITY

"If you ask 3 people what the digital twin is, you get 5 answers. If you ask 3 people what the digital thread is, you get 15 answers."

— Marc Lind, Strategic Vice President at Aras

The purpose of a digital twin is to capture the essence of a physical entity so perfectly in a software model that it performs just like the real-world object for tasks such as monitoring status and exploring operations. In essence, the digital twin simulates real-world scenarios to provide real-world solutions without real-world costs. But there are a lot of definitions of what a digital twin is, including those mirroring a production process,

To understand the definition, consider the parallel to automotive navigation. If you have ever used a paper roadmap paper, you know that such maps are used as a paper twin of atlases that had been used for centuries.

The first virtual roadmap was a dedicated GPS, which gave an unchanging map of the roadways that was similar to paper maps but more compact and could determine a driving route. By purchasing a GPS, you were willing to pay more money to become part of the manufacturer's business model of meeting the customer's need for a regularly updated map or one from a different region. Soon after, a hardwired GPS was replaced by a smartphone app that was more accurate and included traffic lights, road signs, real-time traffic reports, and the locations of restaurants, gas stations, and other stopovers.

It's important to recognize that the digital twin captures the physics of how the device behaves and does not just represent its physical dimensions. For example, a digital twin of a wineglass will shatter when dropped in the virtual environment

Types of Digital Twins

Product twins can function as a faster, cheaper product prototype, much like 3D-printed objects (described in Chapter 10) did previously, but without any physicality. The object's characteristics of the object must be captured and updated as needed to account for the changing needs of the object based on what it has experienced, much like a real object would need to do. For example, if the virtual glass is dropped just a few inches, and it doesn't break, there should still be changes to its physical structure because of the internal stresses it experienced. For example, the glass may not break but the internal stress weakened the glass and the glass ultimately breaks when it is washed in hot water. Another example occurs when an avatar retains the scars and the treasure from previous computer games.

Digital twins can be used in manufacturing operations. Just as product twins can mirror real-world counterparts as unique individuals, digital twins can predict that a part will still be functional even if something unexpected occurs during the manufacturing process.

Process twins create a digital twin of the manufacturing equipment. A process twin can provide an analysis of a real factory problem even before it has been constructed. Process twins can model many scenarios. For example, for processes that require a lot of energy to dry material, such as food, textile, and pulp and paper operations, the process twin can run the material through the line and predict the yield, throughput, and cost. (A video about a process twin in the chemical manufacturing industry can be found in this endnote[25]) .

System twins can model an entire factory and even include the suppliers providing the factory with parts and raw materials. Few system twins exist yet, but they are imminent as the technology is evolving quickly. Digital twins may rely on the other enabling technologies, such as smart sensors, to communicate the status of the system. This would ensure that software twin is accurately modeling the physical system at all times.

From a manufacturing viewpoint, there are three main goals of deploying digital twins.

▸ The first is to cut costs in the engineering and product design phases of a product, system, or factory because digital modifications are much faster to implement.

▸ The second is to provide faster reiterative designs than creating a physical model can, even one created with an additive manufacturing 3D printer.

▸ The third is to save costs by shifting from reactive and preventive maintenance to predictive maintenance. Such savings can be into the billions. One automotive company achieved a 37% reduction in downtime by using a digital twin model to predict future machinery downtime and make repairs in advance of the downtime.[26]

Movies that Feature Digital Twins

The following are just a few recent movies that incorporate digital twins into the story line and illustrate that its often beneficial to be able to manipulate the computer representation of the real thing to gain some sort of advantage:

Iron Man, I, Robot, Click (all digital twins of people). *Apollo 13* used a physical twin to find a solution when the real spacecraft was peril.

Careers in Digital Twins[27]

There is a lot of overlap with the other software positions discussed in prior chapters. They usually require a degree in computer or data science. As the field matures, I expect that job titles reflecting the term digital twins will appear soon.

Discussion Topics

Digital twins are useful in many aspects of Smart Manufacturing, including creating computer models of the factory and the product that is being produced. This has benefits throughout the design, manufacturing, and use of the product

1. How might the digital twin of the roadways affect the progress of autonomous vehicles?
2. What new business opportunities could utilize digital twins?
3. How could digital twins be used in the training of new employees?

Chapter 16:
BLOCKCHAIN: APPLIED MATHEMATICS TO KEEP US HONEST

"The blockchain does one thing: It replaces third-party trust with mathematical proof that something happened."

— Adam Draper, Founder of Boost VC,

If you look up the definition of blockchain, you will read that it is a digital database which is shared within a decentralized network and provides a permanent record of every change or transaction made to it.

Blockchain is rooted in a complex mathematical theory involving cryptography invented by an unknown person in 2008. It is quite the story to learn about if you are interested. Blockchain applications exist when designing, prototyping, and manufacturing a product. It promises to increase transparency throughout the supply chain by tracking and validating authenticity from beginning to end.

I will admit, I was a blockchain skeptic for a long time, much longer than I should have been. The concept that was heavily discussed in the press focused on the applications used by Bitcoin and other cryptocurrencies. To me, it just seemed too far "out there" to have implications for a manufacturing operation. I wasn't alone. In a survey conducted just a short time ago, only 12% of respondents said that the manufacturing sector was leading this technology compared to 46% who said the financial sector was the leader.[28]

Blockchain to Fight Counterfeiting

It may come as a surprise to you that many products can change hands fifty times from the manufacturer to the end user. In the consumer world, an example is the pharmaceuticals that you buy from your local drugstore. They pass through many different wholesalers before reaching you and are often repackaged along the way. The problem is that the controls on both the medicine and the packaging are inadequate, so counterfeiting is a real and deadly concern. Unfortunately, deaths have been caused by fake medicine.[29]

Counterfeiting problems also exist in the manufacturing world as counterfeit electrical components, computer chips, and even fake-branded electrical connectors are often sold as authentic. Counterfeit goods are estimated to cost manufacturers $1.82 trillion per year.

Blockchain is part of a strange sounding but intriguing concept called "zero trust networks." It means that network access is not given to any device until it is authenticated and proves it has a valid reason for the access. This is for devices attempting to gain access from outside the network and for those already inside it, which is a change from how it was previously done.

Traditionally, trust is done at the perimeter of an organization. Think of your house; do you let someone inside who isn't known or trusted? If it's a friend or relative, you let them in. If it's someone you hired to work at your house but you haven't previously met them, you ask to see their ID before allowing them in. The trouble is that once inside, there are no longer any checks. In a network (recall the cybersecurity discussion), once you breach the firewalls and get inside a system, an attacker can move all around to find something to exploit anywhere in the system. For example, in the cyberattack against the retailer Target, hackers got in through the heating and air conditioning controller. In the case of a casino in Las Vegas, the source was a Wi-Fi enabled aquarium heater from a third-party service company.

In a zero-trust network, every request for data must be verified, even if the request comes from inside the organization. Blockchain assists by keeping a permanent record of all transactions and, along with other technologies including artificial intelligence, can identify threats, whether from internal or external sources.

A well-known case of blockchain aside from Bitcoin is the American retailer Walmart, which requires its lettuce supply to be on its blockchain. Each bag of lettuce is traceable from the store back to the farm where it was grown. Every time the lettuce moves to another location, the ledger is updated. In the case of a recall, investigators can examine the ledger to find the source of contamination. If someone tries to substitute other lettuce bags from unapproved sources, the ledger detects the change because it doesn't match the record.

Movies that Feature Blockchain

The following are just a few recent movies that incorporate blockchain into the story line with many of them being documentaries focused on the strange story of how Bitcoin came into existence:

Bitcoin: The End of Money as We Know It, Trust Machine: The Story of Blockchain, The Rise and Fall of Bitcoin, Life on Bitcoin, Banking on Bitcoin, Bitcoin Big Bang, Magic Money: The Bitcoin Revolution, Deep Web

Careers in Blockchain

As with careers in digital twins, these careers also overlap with those described previously in the software section. They usually require a degree in computer or data science, and as the field matures, I expect that job titles reflecting the term blockchain will appear soon.

Discussion Topics

The blockchain may be one of the hardest concepts that I have introduced in this book, but it is finding important uses with Smart Manufacturing operations and the supply chain.

1. What problems can occur when counterfeit products are in the market?
2. How could blockchain be used to verify the authenticity of 3D-printed parts?
3. How could smart sensors that track temperature, time, and location be used with blockchain in shipping operations?

Chapter 17:
SOFTWARE RULES

"A company may employ the most sophisticated software in the world, but unless information is managed, timely, accurate, and complete, the system serves little purpose."

— *Wayne L. Staley, from ERP Lessons Learned* — *Structured Process*

Working in manufacturing means that you will be working with a lot of software and depending upon your position, you will likely be using several different types. There is considerable overlap between software platforms and many connections between different systems. For example, the process control software controlling the equipment will report information to the Manufacturing Execution System (MES), which may also communicate with the enterprise resource platform, or the computer drawing of a part may be accessed by the MES software.

Software markets are highly fragmented and many of the companies specialize in niche industries or applications. So don't be surprised if your employer uses a different system than the ones listed below.

Computer-Aided Design (CAD)

CAD programs allow you to draw 2D and 3D shapes, wiring diagrams, schematics, and nearly anything else that a drawing needs to represent. Libraries of objects enable the designer to drop pieces of equipment into the drawing quickly. The following is a list of popular programs or companies that produce CAD software for manufacturing:

- Solidworks
- Fusion 360
- AutoCA
- Autodesk Inventor
- Rhino 3D
- OnShape
- Bobcad
- Bentley

Computer-Aided Manufacturing (CAM)

CAM software is used to program machines, usually Computer Numerical Control (CNC) machines, to automate a manufacturing process. Used in metal process applications to drill or cut metal, CAM software determines precisely how fast the tools should move, the tool path, and more. The instructions are usually referred to as G-code because it involves programming the geometry of the machine movement. Popular CAM software are the following:

- MasterCAM
- SolidCAM
- EdgeCAM
- HSMWorks
- FeatureCAM
- Gibbscam

Enterprise Resource Systems (ERP)

ERP is used to manage the organization's activities and integrate all the systems into one platform. The goal is to provide information across the organization to ensure that every department is using the same numbers. The ERP ideally connects modules performing different functions such as production, distribution, procurement, accounting, and human resources.

In the movie *Lord of the Rings*, there was one Ring to rule all others. That is what ERP strives to be to all the other software platforms. ERP tends to concentrate on reporting how the company is doing rather than providing control. The data in ERP is often entered by humans rather than done automatically, such as releasing an order that is ready to be shipped.

The market has many vendors but the two with the greatest market share are SAP/Hana and Oracle.

Manufacturing Execution System (MES)

On the plant floor, MES provides real-time and precise control of the manufacturing process. It provides alerts to order more inventory and schedule machine maintenance. Much of the data in MES systems are generated automatically from machines and controllers updating the current status.

Discrete manufacturing uses MES software the most (see Chapter 5 for a refresher on that term) compared to the process industries. It is an extremely fragmented market with vendors supplying small niche applications. The chances are that your company will use an MES different than the ones listed here but these are some of more common ones in the U.S.

▸ IMCO-CIMAG
▸ Aegis FactoryLogix MES
▸ Solumina MES
▸ IQMS Production Scheduling
▸ SyteLine
▸ E2 Shop System
▸ Katana
▸ Infor Visual

Product Lifecycle Management (PLM) Software

PLM organizes the product from the time it begins life as an idea to the time it is discontinued and no longer exists. PLM strives to increase efficiency and reduce development time by linking all product information together.

For example, a product drawn in a CAD program links to the bill of materials (BoM), which is needed to make the product. If the design changes, the BoM changes automatically. This eliminates buying the wrong parts for the product. Makers of PLM software include the following:

▸ Dassault Systems
▸ Autodesk
▸ Siemens PLM
▸ Synopsys
▸ Ansys
▸ Cadence Design Systems
▸ Hexagon
▸ PTC
▸ AVEVA Group

Process Control and Automation Software

For discrete manufacturing operations using programmable logic controllers (PLCs), the software generally comes from the same company that provides the hardware. You are most likely to encounter Rockwell Automation or Siemens because they have the dominant market share in North America, but others include:

▸ Mitsubishi
▸ Schneider Electric
▸ Omron
▸ GE

For process manufacturing, such as in oil and gas, chemical, or pharmaceutical manufacturing, distributed control systems (DCSs) manage the process. The manufacturer of the DCS usually supplies the software as well. The following are several of the most common companies making DCS systems:

▸ ABB
▸ Honeywell Process Solutions
▸ Siemens
▸ Yokogawa Electric
▸ Emerson Automation
▸ Schneider Electric
▸ Rockwell Automation
▸ General Electric

Customer Relationships Manager (CRM)

Finally, it is essential to have a system in place to organize customer information. Addresses, telephone numbers, contacts, sales history, and communication notes are all necessary to ensure that you provide a good customer experience. Ideally, the CRM captures all communications and data about the customer for future reference.

By far, the largest supplier of CRM software is Salesforce. Others include:

- SAP
- Oracle
- Microsoft
- Adobe

There is no doubt that software will continue to increase in importance in Smart Manufacturing. Some of the user interfaces seem as if they were designed in the 1970s and take a long time to learn. Others are modern, intuitive to use, and require no specific training. Many platforms have specially written apps for mobile devices and have been moving to the cloud to enable access to information from anywhere.

I will leave this topic with a joke about how complexity of software is increasing:

"I have always wished for my computer to be as easy to use as my telephone; my wish has come true because I can no longer figure out how to use my telephone."

> — *Bjarne Stroustrup, Computer Scientist known for creating the C++ (pronounced "C sharp sharp) programming language*

Careers in Software

Software systems in Smart Manufacturing plants are complex and there are usually departments dedicated to keeping the systems operational apart from the positions that use software to create products or program machines.

IT Support Specialist provides assistance in setting up computers and software for other employees to use and may function as a member of the help desk when problems arise. wo years of experience, The position typically requires an associate's degree, relevant certificates, and two years of experience. Typical salary is currently $50-70k

Network Administrator installs and troubleshoots the network and creates a system to maintain the availability of the network to all users. The position typically require a bachelor's degree and two years of experience. Typical salary is currently $75-$100k.

Director, Vice President, or Chief Information Officer are the highest levels of managers within a company. These positions typically require an advanced degree and several years of relevant experience. Typical salary is currently $150,000 and beyond.

Discussion Topics

Smart manufacturers use many types of software systems to provide guidance to human workers and to perform specific functions. You can expect to work with at least one of them on a daily basis regardless of your job title.

1. What software would those involved in engineering probably use the most?

2. What software would those involved in accounting and finance be most likely to use?

3. What software would those in sales and marketing use?

SECTION VI:
FINAL THOUGHTS ON THE HUMAN ELEMENT

Chapter 18:

SOFT SKILLS NEVER GO OUT OF FASHION, BUT YOU HAVE TO KEEP UP

"Your attitude, not your aptitude, will determine your altitude."

— *Zig Ziglar, Motivational speaker, author, and salesperson*

Most of this book is on technologies, operations, and processes involved in Smart Manufacturing. But it is not an accident that I include a chapter on soft skills. If you do not have these skills, nothing else matters.

Soft skills used to be defined as being dependable and able to communicate clearly. The definition has evolved to include creativity, critical thinking, emotional intelligence, communication, active learning, decision making, leadership, diversity, cultural intelligence, empathy, change mentality, thought agility, and grit. The following graphic includes yet more characteristics of soft skills:

In the winter of 2016, I participated in a National Academy of Engineering meeting that devoted a significant amount of time to soft skills and, specifically, how to foster them in young engineers. Emotional intelligence was a key subject discussed. It refers to the ability to control and manage your own emotions and recognize how they might affect your behavior. It also means being aware of other's emotional states and the effect on their behavior.

Self-Motivation
Soft Skills for
Problem
Solving
Autonomy
Smart Manufacturing
Cultural   Grit   Adaptability   Responsibility
Sensitivity   Creativity
Reputation   Team Spirit
Growth Mindset   Emotional   Leadership
Awareness   Connection
Persistence
Resourcefulness
Foresight   Conflict   Verbal   Ethics
Etiquette   Resolution   Communications
Non-Verbal
Communication   Coaching   Professionalism

Leadership skills are also crucial at all employee levels and must be developed for any position in Smart Manufacturing. The reason is that in advanced manufacturing and many other technical fields, no one will give you hour-to-hour or even day-to-day tasks to complete. The organizational structures of most companies have become flatter, meaning all employees are expected to identify problems and lead others towards solutions.

Critical Thinking Skills

According to the World Economic Forum, critical thinking skills are essential for all humans. After all, we have learned that robots, computers, and artificial intelligence are taking over the jobs and tasks that don't require critical thinking so the added value that humans bring to the workplace is the ability to think critically and creatively.

In a new Smart Manufacturing position, you will be expected to take ownership of the responsibilities of your position and start making a difference within a short time by understanding the company's goals and driving toward them, often without explicit directions on how to do so. It used to be that only engineers were considered the problem solvers of their organizations, but that isn't true anymore. Organizations can't afford someone in upper management pointing out all the problems and ordering them to be solved. All employees need to be problem identifiers and then solvers.

Success in the field requires grit and the drive to be proactive and make changes. Employers need a higher percentage of people fully engaged because it is employee engagement that can make or break a company.

I actually suggest putting the term soft skills aside and replacing it with durable skills. I believe that durable is a better term because these are the skills that will last your entire career. We know that many hard skills have a short shelf life because one technology is inevitably replaced by another technology, like the FORTRAN computer programming language I learned in college. Durable skills will take you far, probably more than anything else in your career. Develop a robust set of these skills and at least one hard skill and you will have a great job in Smart Manufacturing or any industry.

Movies that Feature Soft Skills

The following are just a few recent movies that incorporate soft skills into the story line, showing how mastering or lacking them can affect the success of the individual or results for the enterprise:

The Pursuit of Happyness, Rain Man, E.T. the Extra-Terrestrial, Any Given Sunday, Apollo 13, Kung Fu Panda, McFarland, USA

Careers in Soft Skills

Exhibiting mastery of soft skills not only helps you get that first job but is critical for advancing in your career and winning promotions. Exhibiting an exceptional ability to work, and lead, others is one of the most sought-after traits, especially at the higher management levels.

Executive Management is usually defined as director and above levels, including president. vice presidents, and directors. These positions are responsible for determining "what" should be done rather than "how" and are focused on the future to ensure the company meets its goals as business conditions and customer needs change.

Senior Management is usually defined as the director or manager level. It is common for teams to report to each senior management position. The key focus of the position is to provide input to executive management on the "how" to achieve the company's goals.

Production Supervisor or Manager oversees the plant floor. These positions typically require a college degree or 2-5 years of experience as an operator plus demonstrated leadership skills. Typical salary is currently $40-80k.

Human Resources is involved in designing systems and programs that maximize the ability of all employees to perform at their highest levels. Human resources positions can also be responsible for recruiting new employees into the company and to ensure that all policies comply with regulatory requirements.

Discussion Topics

Effective use of soft skills enables human workers to achieve individually and as a member of a team. Soft skills are increasingly important as the human job roles continue to shift from simple, repetitive tasks to those requiring creativity and flexibility.

1. Discuss what "responsibility" means to you.
2. What are examples of positive and negative "nonverbal communication" in the workplace
3. Why is the "cultural sensitivity" important to American manufacturers?

Chapter 19:
GETTING INTO MANUFACTURING

I hope that you are now very excited about a career in manufacturing. Great, welcome aboard! But how do you get your foot in the door?

Several paths will lead to a career in Smart Manufacturing. There is no one right path. And none of these paths are final. The first path you take won't seal your life forever in one direction. Depending on your stage in life, deciding what to study or where to work may seem overwhelming and you may worry that your whole future hangs in the balance.

My recommendation is to pick a direction and start moving. As the saying goes, "A moving car is easier to steer than a parked car" because once you are active and pursuing an idea, dream, or career path, you can make adjustments along the way. Plus, once you are moving, you get to see beyond the bend in the road that was impossible to see from your starting point.

What are some of the paths you may take? These generally fall into four-year degree programs (or four-year degree plus master's degree), two-year degree programs, and the plant floor approach.

The Four-Year University Degree

A bachelor's (or bachelor's plus master's) degree is a path to manufacturing. There is no one major that is best. There are many to choose from depending upon your particular interests and talents. Think of it as a starting point, not an ending. Almost any college major can provide an entry path into a manufacturer or a supplier of one of the enabling technologies. I have known many people in highly technical positions with degrees in business, social science, or even the arts.

If you want to start designing equipment, a product, or systems right away, I suggest you pursue a STEM-based major and, specifically, engineering or computer science. Mechanical engineering is the most common choice. A 2018 blog by *Interesting Engineering* listed the popularity of engineering degrees as follows[30]:

1. Mechanical Engineering
2. Electrical Engineering
3. Civil Engineering
4. Chemical Engineering
5. Computer Engineering
6. Biomedical Engineering
7. Industrial Engineering

If you are interested in designing equipment or a product, mechanical engineering is the most popular choice because it covers a broad array of subjects. Do not underestimate the value of being able to create drawings and so you should spend time honing your proficiency long before you enter an engineering program.

If designing integrated systems seems more appealing to you, consider industrial engineering as this major offers greater focus on the operation, including manufacturing, resource planning, and quality control. Some schools name this major as manufacturing engineering.

Almost every chapter in this book shows how computer technology shapes manufacturing, so computer engineering or computer science is a pathway. A position in big data or blockchain will be more accessible with such a degree.

If you decide to obtain a university degree, find a school that will provide you with hands-on experience in designing and implementing a real project as part of your coursework or provides an internship at the earliest possible point and no later than sometime in the sophomore year.

By the way, almost any hands-on skill will set you apart in your career path, no matter which degree you earn. A mechanical engineer with a four-year degree, that's good. A mechanical engineer with a certificate in welding, even better!

The Two-Year College Degree

Sometimes called community, junior, or technical colleges, the two-year program is one of the most under-rated paths into manufacturing and careers in general. The two-year degree offers many advantages. I will begin with what you will learn. It is primarily a skills-based education and from day one, you start using the tools of the trade. As employers are always looking for those who can get the job done, get things fixed, and keep things moving, this advantage will set you apart from other job candidates.

Positions in industrial maintenance, mechatronics, and mechanical tech are just a few that are available to those with a two-year degree. The cost of earning a two-year degree is typically a fraction of what a four-year degree costs.

Although a two-year degree may be all you need, I would still encourage you to consider the ease of transferring credits if you decide to continue with a four-year degree. Although all colleges and universities accept transfer credit, some two-year institutions have agreements with universities that make it easier to transfer credits. If you already hold a position, many larger employers will also contribute to the cost of your education because of the benefit to building your skills.

Plant Floor Approach: Right Into the Workplace

If you must find work immediately, this is where your soft skills can pay off. Your goal is to convince the prospective employer that you can do the job, do it correctly and professionally, and be dependable. You only have one chance to make that first impression, so I suggest that you practice answering potential interview questions with someone who will give you honest feedback. Interviewers tend to have predictable questions that you can find on the Internet, so be prepared with your answers. An online search will not only provide you lists of questions but also the best approach for answering them.

Keep in mind the most important soft skills, such as grit discussed in the last chapter. Consider how to set yourself aside from the other candidates so that you rise to the top of the list. If you haven't heard back, email or give them a call.

Whether you come to an interview with a four-year degree, two-year degree, or high school diploma, research the mission and goals of the company and be able to express how you can help achieve them. Be prepared to ask them questions that demonstrate your preparation for the interview, For example, asking questions about plans to incorporate additive manufacturing into their factory will show how well you understand the company. But remember that the interview questions aren't designed to discuss your personal story if it doesn't relate to the position. It's to show how your particular set of skills will help them achieve their business goals.

Networking

Finally, you should network in your local and regional manufacturing community. There are several ways to make networking connections.

Every state runs a manufacturing extension program, almost always abbreviated MEP. Look up the MEP for your state online and participate in the next scheduled meeting or conference. The cost may be free or quite modest but if it is more than you can afford, contact the organizer, explain that you are a student and interested in manufacturing in the local community, and ask if you can attend free of charge. In my experience, you will likely get a free pass for at least the first meeting.

Another opportunity to network is Manufacturing Week, which occurs in October every year. Find out which manufacturers are opening their doors to the public that day. Dress at least a notch or two above how you usually would, be prepared to ask good questions, and let them know that you would be interested in working for them. They could have a hundred resumes of people hoping to land a position with the company but by engaging with current employees and managers face-to-face, you can make an impression, so make it count!

Many colleges hold job fairs with employers looking for students about to graduate. But even if you are only part-way through your education, you could attend and try to land an internship. Just another way of standing out from the crowd!

If you are enrolled in specific engineering or vocational discipline, there are professional societies that meet regularly in your area! For the electrical and computer science professions, the IEEE is the biggest while for mechanical engineering, the ASME has the most members. They generally welcome students who take the extra step to reach out and engage with them and some have dedicated student chapters with reduced dues.

Discussion Topics

Getting stared in manufacturing means taking that first step and making yourself known to the community. If you have read this book you already have a "Big Picture" understanding of what Smart Manufacturing entails and you should use it to your advantage.

1. If you are a high-school student, what sort of job do you see yourself enjoying in the future?
2. If you are considering an educational institution, research which ones have the most hands-on training or internship opportunities. Does this appeal to you?
3. How can you use the information presented in this book to show employers that you would be an exceptional employee?

CONCLUSION

The dark, dirty, and dangerous environments associated with production plants no longer represent the modern factory or Smart Manufacturing operations. Over the last few decades, serious misunderstandings about the importance and value of manufacturing, especially at the federal level, created policies that accelerated factory closures in the U.S. and spurred wage stagnation.

Smart Manufacturing and Industry 4.0 have changed this picture dramatically. Automating routine tasks, both physical and mental, takes unnecessary human labor costs out of the question of "Where should my manufacturing facility be located?" When that happens, the economic equation changes and the answer becomes:

▶ Near the most reliable and inexpensive energy sources.
▶ Close to the best transportation networks.
▶ Accessible to the best communication systems.
▶ Or simply, where I am closest to my customer.

Automation eliminates some jobs, creates others, and changes nearly all of them. This shifting job landscape requires reskilling and upskilling but also provides many opportunities for workers. Automation takes routine, robot-like tasks off human workers and frees them to use more creativity and reflection in their work.

Mass customization of the product is the guiding philosophy when it comes to Smart Manufacturing. The trend is moving quickly toward personalized products and not mass production for the masses. The goal of Industry 4.0 is explicitly to produce a product in lot sizes of one, which means a single item, not a pack, case, or carton.

The emphasis on personalized products also provides comprehensive sociological benefits as well. Consider the amount of waste generated by mass-produced clothing as an example.

That "fast fashion" shirt that retails for $10 in a U.S. shop may contain Indian cotton, sent to Bangladesh for fabric production, then sent to Europe for final assembly, before finally arriving in New York or other destinations for purchase by the consumer. As not all of those mass-produced shirts will sell, what happens to them? Unsold merchandise is often destroyed, such as the billions of dollars worth of clothing that was incinerated by one retailer[31].

Producing for a single consumer will significantly reduce the waste stream. Even better than recycling is not to produce items in the first place, conserve the energy used to transport the parts and finished products worldwide, and avoid the costs of maintaining buildings that store and sell these products.

Many of the chapters on emerging technologies illustrate that manufacturing is as complex and advanced as any other industry. Technologies are applied to create efficiencies and higher-quality output. In nearly every chapter, I reference other technologies to show just how interconnected the manufacturing system is. Smart Manufacturing is less of a tangible and more of a mindset. Robots performing movements determined by artificial intelligence and communicating securely to clients with blockchain are happening now.

Smart Manufacturing flattens organizational hierarchies as the workforce incorporates different and highly specialized expertise who must collaborate in a system. The types of soft skills needed at all levels within an organization is increasing with critical thinking being the most crucial mindset but others also important to success. To thrive in Smart Manufacturing, I can't emphasize enough how important it is to hone your soft skills just as vigorously as your technological skills.

If you are looking for a career that builds the future, a career in Smart Manufacturing may be right for you! In this book, I offer just the briefest of introductions to the scope of work and careers you can pursue in Smart Manufacturing. Do your research and discover which facet of manufacturing resonates most with you.

If you are a parent, teacher, or counselor, I hope that I have provided enough information for you to be comfortable recommending manufacturing to young people looking for a career path. And if you are a more experienced worker looking to leave service or retail sector jobs, there are paths for you as well.

FURTHER READING RECOMMENDATIONS

1. *Maximizing Job-Creation Bang-for-Buck by Reducing Import Leakages* by Josh Bivens, published in June 2019, discusses how large U.S. infrastructure projects could spur manufacturing as long as there is a "Buy American" mandate. Available at: https://www.epi.org/publication/maximizing-job-creation-bang-for-buck-by-reducing-import-leakages-how-many-more-jobs-would-be-supported-by-infrastructure-investments-if-import-shares-were-lower-in-domestic-manufacturing/

2. *Does America Really Need Manufacturing?* by Gary P. Pisano and Willy C. Shig, published in the March 2012 *Harvard Business Review*. Eight years before COVID-19 and the resulting manufacturing shortages, the authors concluded that "policymakers must abandon that experiment now [referring to the reduction of manufacturing capability in the United States] — before it's too late." Available at: https://hbr.org/2012/03/does-america-really-need-manufacturing

3. Digital Supply Networks: Transform Your Supply Chain And Gain Competitive Advantage With Disruptive Technology And Reimagined Processes was published in 2020 by Amit Sinha, Ednilson Bernardes, Rafael Calderon, and Thorsten Wuest, who are all industry-oriented academics who understand how new technologies will affect supply chain management. Available at: https://www.mhprofessional.com/9781260458190-usa-digital-supply-networks-transform-your-supply-chain-and-gain-competitive-advantage-with-disruptive-technology-and-reimagined-processes-group

4. *Supply Chain Management for Dummies, 2nd edition* was published in 2020 by Daniel Stanton, known as "Mr. Supply Chain." He addresses the subject in a fun and engaging manner. Available at: https://www.dummies.com/business/management/supply-chain-management-dummies-cheat-sheet/

5. *Making Value for America. Embracing the Future of Manufacturing, Technology, and Work."* Published in 2015 by the National Academies of Sciences, Engineering, Medicine, this book offers an excellent historical study of American manufacturing coupled with a forward-looking perspective and direction for manufacturing in the U.S. Available at: https://www.nae.edu/129940/Making-Value-for-America

6. *Manufacturing Workforce Development Playbook. Preparing for the Manufacturing Renaissance in America* was edited by Keith S. Campbell and published in 2014, This book focuses on technical education at the two-year college level. A sample chapter subheading is "Building Awareness About How Cool Manufacturing Is." How cool is that? Available at: https://www.nist.gov/system/files/documents/2017/04/28/Manufacturing_Workforce_Dev_Playbook.pdf

7. *Recommendations for Implementing the Strategic Initiative INDUSTRIE 4.0: Final Report of the Industrie 4.0 Working Group* by Henning Kagermann, Wolfgang Wahlster, and Johannes Helbig, and published in 2013. Germany created the public relations-friendly and catchy term Industry 4.0 to describe Smart Manufacturing. I urge you to read the last section, "Example Application 5: Sudden Change of Supplier During the Production Due to a Crisis Beyond the Manufacturer's Control" for an eerie forecast of the material shortages caused by COVID-19 seven years after being published. Available at: https://www.din.de/blob/76902/e8cac883f42bf28536e7e8165993f1fd/recommendations-for-implementing-industry-4-0-data.pdf

ABOUT THE AUTHOR

Mike Nager has an electronics engineering degree and more than twenty years of experience working for leading German and American manufacturers of industrial automation and connection device technologies. He's consulted with hundreds of manufacturers and utilities to design more efficient, environmentally friendly, responsive plants and factories.

He was named a 2020 Top 10 IIoT Influencer by Onalytica and has published dozens of trade publications.

Among his many projects, he has installed sensors inside the massive machine tools used in making automotive engines, tested industrial radio technology deep underground in the New York subways, and wore a cleanroom suit to work with clients onsite in both the pharmaceutical and semiconductor industries.

Mike was the keynote speaker in 2018 at the Nevada Economic Development Conference and in 2019 at the Réseau Innovation 4.0 Network in Quebec. He has presented at numerous conferences hosted by organizations and conferences, including the following:

▶ IoT Emerge Conference
▶ Connecting Electronics Industries Association
▶ International Society for Pharmaceutical Engineering
▶ International Institute of Electrical Engineers
▶ Information and Communications Technology Conference
▶ Material Handling Industry Association
▶ International Society of Automation
▶ Association of Career and Technical Education

Mike is a volunteer with the IEEE Mini-Engineering Academy that provides high school students opportunities to work with engineers on hands-on projects in many areas. He is an advisory board member to several educational institutions, including the Monmouth County Vocational School District and the Metropolitan Education District.

He lives at the Jersey Shore with his fantastic wife, two daughters, and one ugly rescue dog.

ENDNOTES

1 https://www.nytimes.com/2011/08/28/magazine/does-america-need-manufacturing.html

2 https://theconversation.com/the-giant-sucking-sound-of-nafta-ross-perot-was-ridiculed-as-alarmist-in-1992-but-his-warning-turned-out-to-be-prescient-120258

3 https://read.oecd-ilibrary.org/employment/automation-skills-use-and-training_2e2f4eea-en#page61

4 https://www.nae.edu/129940/Making-Value-for-America

5 https://www.fastcompany.com/3041953/american-giant-guns-for-gap-by-doubling-down-on-us-of-a

6 https://www.smartmanufacturinginitiative.com/2013/05/17/the-three-camps-of-manufacturing-part-1/

7 https://www.forbes.com/sites/realspin/2017/01/09/time-for-washington-to-think-like-a-state/#5e81220b30a3

8 https://www.inc.com/eric-markowitz/exposing-the-great-myths-about-american-manufacturing.html

9 https://www.nytimes.com/2018/03/27/business/hm-clothes-stock-sales.html

10 https://www.slideshare.net/MikeNager/ieee-conference-industrial-ethernet

11   https://www.wired.com/2014/11/countdown-to-zero-day-stuxnet/

12   https://www.brookings.edu/blog/the-avenue/2015/04/29/dont-blame-the-robots-for-lost-manufacturing-jobs/

13   https://www.nytimes.com/2017/09/10/technology/amazon-robots-workers.html

14   https://www.wired.com/2010/01/0125robot-kills-worker/

15   https://make.3dexperience.3ds.com/processes/material-jetting

16   https://www.aersale.com/media-center/beat-fleet-downtime-costs-with-integrated-mro-solutions#:~:text=Several%20airlines%20have%20publicly%20reported,%24200%20million%20for%20Q1%202019

17   https://www.wired.com/story/massive-ai-powered-robots-are-3d-printing-entire-rockets/?utm_source=twitter&utm_medium=social&utm_campaign=onsite-share&utm_brand=wired&utm_social-type=earned

18   https://www.bbvaopenmind.com/en/technology/digital-world/iot-implementation-and-challenges/

19   https://www.rasmussen.edu/degrees/technology/blog/big-data-jobs-in-big-demand/

20   https://media.ford.com/content/fordmedia/fna/us/en/news/2015/07/16/ford-reduces-production-line-injury-rate-by-70-percent.html

21   https://circuitstream.com/blog/xr-jobs-in-demand/

22   https://www.rev.com/blog/artificial-intelligence-vs-machine-learning-whats-the-difference

23   https://xkcd.com/1875/

24   https://www.northeastern.edu/graduate/blog/career-in-artificial-intelligence/ for more information.

25   https://www.bentley.com/en/products/product-line/digital-twins/plantsight

26   https://www.challenge.org/insights/digital-twin-genie-in-manufacturing/

27   https://www.challenge.org/insights/digital-twin-jobs/

28   https://www.pwc.com/us/en/industries/industrial-products/library/blockchain-industrial-manufacturing.html#:~:text=From%20sourcing%20raw%20materials%20delivering,Materials%20provenance%20and%20counterfeit%20detection

29   https://www.ncbi.nlm.nih.gov/pmc/articles/PMC4105729/

30   https://interestingengineering.com/the-most-popular-engineering-majors-in-the-us

31   https://www.vox.com/the-goods/2018/9/17/17852294/fashion-brands-burning-merchandise-burberry-nike-h-and-m

Made in USA - Kendallville, IN
1233233_9781736362518
02.15.2021 1246